Family friendly working

Inspiring ideas for making money when you have kids

Antonia Chitty

Editor Roni Jay

WHITE LADDER PRESS

new tricks for old dogs

Published by White Ladder Press Ltd

Great Ambrook, Near Ipplepen, Devon TQ12 5UL

01803 813343

www.whiteladderpress.com

First published in Great Britain in 2008

10 9 8 7 6 5 4 3 2 1

13-digit ISBN 978 1 905410 26 2

British Library Cataloguing in Publication Data

A CIP record for this book can be obtained from the British Library.

Designed and typeset by Julie Martin Ltd
Cover photos by Jonathon Bosley
Cover design by Julie Martin Ltd
Printed and bound by TJ International Ltd, Padstow, Cornwall
Cover printed by St Austell Printing Company

Printed on totally chlorine-free paper
The paper used for the text pages of this book is FSC certified.
FSC (The Forest Stewardship Council) is an international
network to promote responsible management of the world's forests.

FSC

Mixed Sources
Product group from well-managed
forests and other controlled sources

Cert no. SGS-COC-2482
www.fsc.org
© 1996 Forest Stewardship Council

 White Ladder books are distributed in the UK by Virgin Books

White Ladder Press
Great Ambrook, Near Ipplepen, Devon TQ12 5UL
01803 813343
www.whiteladderpress.com

Contents

Introduction

This book is all about finding ways to work and still have the time you want to spend with your family. You've probably already found out that life with kids means that you are perpetually short of time, and the money doesn't seem to last until the end of the month. Or maybe you have far too much time on your hands and would love to have something more interesting to do.

Using the experience of more than a hundred parents who have found creative ways round the problems, this book is packed with solutions and inspiring ideas to make your working life more family friendly. There is no easy solution, and you will still find that there are not enough hours in the day, but if you're looking for something beyond the nine-to-five, you will find hundreds of helpful ideas.

Chapter 1

Finding ways to work

This first chapter will help you assess your strengths, skills and motivation. By reading this you will be able to work out more easily which of the ideas in the following chapters will suit you and fit with your family and circumstances. There is also information about employment and self-employment, and a guide to your rights if you have a job but want to change your hours to fit with the family.

Why do you want to work?

Before you start looking for ideas, take a moment to work out what you are looking for. Why do you want to work? Is it purely financial necessity? Whatever your work, would you rather be at home with the children every day? Emma says, "I didn't want to go back to work at all, and we managed for a while, but I've just started working evenings because otherwise we can't pay all the bills at the end of the month."

Or do you desperately need to do something that involves adult conversation? Will one more episode of the Teletubbies tip you over the edge? Elaine, mum to Tim, now eight, says, "I remember the moment when, sitting in the lounge one afternoon, I just felt I was going to run out of the house screaming. I was going slowly mad, sitting here watching CBeebies with Tim, and I needed desperately to find something more interesting to do, at least some of the time."

 Tim decided that he'd put his career second when his daughter was a baby. His father had had a busy job and he remembers seeing very little of him as a child, so when his father died when Tim was still quite young, he was left with a real desire to be around for his children. Tim's daughter is now a teenager, and he has two sons aged six and one. Tim says, "I now work some evenings and weekends as a musician. I'm able to take my older son to school, and play in the park with the little one." Tim's partner Charlotte is self-employed too. Tim says, "Working this way means we don't have lots of money, but I love my days with the children. We don't have a car, and try to get second-hand clothes and furniture, but it's more important to me to know I'm a big part of my children's' lives."

When can you work?

Before you rush off to the JobCentre, think about when it would suit you best to work. Take into account factors such as whether you are good at early mornings or better at late nights. Are your children at school, and who could drop them off or pick them up if you weren't available? Do you have friends or family members who could take turns with collecting and dropping children off? Or can you offer evenings, weekends and bank holidays? And even if you are planning on working while your little ones nap, think about how you will fit in the other jobs you might normally have done in this time. Don't just think about how the cleaning and washing is going to get done. You also need some time for yourself and for your partner and this can easily get shoved aside.

 Nadine Lewis found the decision to quit her job after the birth of her twins and work from home was almost made for her. She had returned to work after the birth of her first child, Abby, and loved her career in HR. She says, "It was different with three children under the age of three. Childcare cost me £22 each child per day. I worked three days a week, and although I would have got a discount on the fees if I had gone full time I valued the days with the kids too much. My job seemed well paid, but I just couldn't afford to return to work, pay the cost of travel, clothes and lunches, income tax, NI and so on. I would have been working for negative income." Nadine started to work from home as a virtual assistant, but then came up with an idea for an emergency ID card for children. She now works full-time at her company, IdentifyMe, which makes a range of ID solutions.

Where can you work?

The location of your work is limited by whether you have time where you do not have to look after the kids. If they are of school age, this is simpler, and you may be able to look for work out of the house during school hours. If you have pre-schoolers, do you have someone who could look after the children if you got a job, or would you get childcare? There are lots of jobs that you could do during the evenings and weekends if you have a partner or family member who could help out with childcare, and that way you do not incur further costs. Alternatively, you may want to limit yourself to things you can do in the home. This has many advantages: you gain time by avoiding travelling; you can pop another load of washing on or put dinner in the oven while you are working; and you do not have so much disruption when children are sick. You do have to be more creative about making the opportunity to work, and disciplined enough not to just put your feet up and watch TV. This book will help you with lots of ideas whether you are restricted to working from your house or can look for a job beyond the home.

What are your strengths?

Knowing your strengths will help you find a job or create a business that you love. Take some time to assess what you like doing. Look at the skills you used in past employment. And look at what you enjoy doing now. If you are short of ideas, ask friends and family what they think are your strengths. Maybe you are well organised, good at looking after people, physically strong, or love being creative.

Note down these qualities in four columns, as below:

Skills I've used in previous jobs/ use currently (eg typing, good at ironing etc.)	My qualifications and certificates	What I enjoy doing (eg keeping fit, crafts, writing etc)	My other strengths (eg organisation, sensitive to others' feelings, etc)

Draw a circle around some of the qualities which stand out to you, and refer back to these when you are looking at the different ideas for jobs and businesses in the following chapters. Will each opportunity allow you to work when and where suits you, and will it use the skills and qualities you have?

 Sharon Russell was a paediatric nurse but found she was depressed and lonely after quitting her career to be a full-time mum. She decided a job would get her out of the house and give her something interesting to do. She worked out carefully what she wanted. Her four requirements for a job were: something with children, but not clinical nursing; something part-time or flexible; something close to home, and something that would get her out and about. Sharon scoured the job ads, and was delighted to find a job with a charity called Brainwave. Sharon now works supporting children with special needs with a programme of exercises to do at home. She does 18 hours a week and can plan her own hours to fit with her family and her clients' needs. Unusually, her son's nursery is open seven days a week, which fits well with Sharon's work patterns. She says, "My husband works shifts, and so some weeks we both work weekends and have days off mid-week. When my son starts school I will fit my 18 hours around school days. I love my job; it suits everything I need at this time in my life."

What resources can you commit?

If you want to start a business you need to invest time and resources. What you will need depends on what you aim to do, so have a look at your resources now so you can plan ahead.

If you want to work from home, you will need a space to work in. Although the kitchen table may seem like a good place to start, you won't get far if you have to clear away your work every time someone needs to eat, the kids want to paint or do homework, or you have visitors over. Try to have a small table or desk, or cupboard or corner, depending on what you want to do, that is just for your work. If you have a study or office, even better. Make sure that there is a place you can leave your work safely. It is inevitable that you will get interrupted. Businesses with stock need storage space, whether you are running your own business or selling items for another company as a rep.

After taking voluntary redundancy, Kim Larrad was looking for something she could do while being at home with her two small children. She bumped into a former colleague of her partner's, and discovered that she had a business for sale which her husband had run until his death. The business was selling wooden, traditional and natural toys, which Kim felt fitted perfectly with her family and interests. She says, "I remember lying awake all night thinking that would be so perfect as a business to run from home. I worked out if I could afford to use my redundancy money to buy the business. I got back in touch with her straight away the next morning and the deal was agreed." Kim has been running Toy Giant since 2003.

Use of a computer

Access to a computer is almost essential nowadays. If you're a computer virgin, look in the local library, JobCentre or community centre for free courses to get you started with computer skills. If you need to use the computer to get together a curriculum vitae to apply for jobs there may be courses for this too. Libraries and community centres often now offer computer access as part of their services, or you can use an internet café if you think you will only need the computer occasionally. If you are running a business you will soon find that a computer has many uses. It will help when drawing up a business plan if you can use one of the many templates online, and there are programmes to make invoices and accounts simple – everything is set up for you to enter your business's details. Later on in the book we will look at more ways to make money with a computer, but for now just think about how you can get access to a computer and acquire some basic skills if you have none.

Other equipment

If you are planning on making something to sell, what sort of equipment will you need? Work out how much this will cost, and whether what you have is up to the job. For example, a domestic sewing machine may be fine for occasional work, but if you are sewing for a few hours each day, you may want to look at upgrading to an industrial model. As well as purchasing equipment, you may want further funds to get your enterprise started, buy into a franchise, or purchase an existing business. And you will need money to promote and market your business to attract customers.

Bex Smith started her business almost by accident. She was always handy at making things, and when she decided to use cloth nappies it seemed like a good idea to see if she could save a few pounds and sew them herself. Since then she has designed and made a range of eco-friendly baby products and sells them wholesale and through her website **www.nappymat.co.uk**. Bex says, "I used my domestic sewing machine for a while, but I now have several different bits of industrial level equipment to cope with the amount of sewing I do."

Doing it alone?

If you are thinking about some of the business ideas in the forthcoming chapters, you will also need to work out what sort of support you will need. Talk to your partner as your new enterprise will take up time you previously spent with them and the family. Are they supportive of your idea? You may find that they are initially enthusiastic but start to complain when they realise your business will take time, energy and possibly financial investment. Try to keep them updated on your progress, as you will find a supportive family invaluable.

Working together

You may want to go into business with someone else. If you are considering working with a friend, it is vital to thrash out details in advance. How will you divide jobs neither of you want to do, how will initial costs be split and what will happen to any profit? Read on for a practical guide to the differences between employment, self-employment, partnerships and companies.

Ways to work

It's pretty straightforward if you work for someone else. You are employed, and they pay you after deducting tax and National Insurance. If you are thinking about working for yourself, it is important to decide whether you want to work alone as a sole trader, form a partnership, or set up a company. There are financial implications to consider and, whichever way you work, it is wise to talk to the Inland Revenue. Here we spell out some of the pros and cons of different ways to work.

Self-employment

The simplest way to start out is to register as self-employed.

Call the Inland Revenue within three months of starting your business. When you are self-employed, you receive all the income and profits from your business and you are responsible for debts if the business fails. You are taxed on the profits your business makes but can claim your business expenses against your tax. If your income is low you can request to be exempt from National Insurance payments, but it is wise to make voluntary class two payments of just a few pounds each week to retain your entitlement to benefits such as maternity allowance.

Partnerships

If you plan to work with someone else, you are 'in partnership'. Get a solicitor to draw up an agreement outlining how the business is shared. You are likely to still need to register as self-employed, and have the same responsibilities and benefits as above. Profits are shared as you have agreed in the document forming the partnership.

Limited liability partnership is a relatively new arrangement that means your personal assets are not at stake if the business fails. Similar to registering a company, you have to register limited liability partnerships at Companies House.

Partnership has its pros and cons. One mum who ran a business with a partner says, "The ups were I had somebody to share idea with and to act as a sounding board. She also brought specialist knowledge to the business. On the downside, she didn't do her share of the work. Often I'd think she was dealing with things and she didn't follow it through. She didn't fill in her partner's tax return form, and I have been liable for the fines. This has caused me a lot of stress, and I have lost a friend. We have dissolved the partnership and I would avoid partnership working after my experience."

Companies

You may want to set up a limited liability company. Register at Companies House for this. There are many firms who will set up a company for you for a fee, in the region of a couple of hundred pounds. Some enterprise agencies can provide assistance too. Running your business as a company protects your personal assets if the business fails. You would be employed by the company and taxed through PAYE on your income. You will probably also have shares in the company and receive dividends on the profits. If operating as a company, you do need an accountant, and have to submit annual accounts to Companies House. You will be a company director. A company can be sold more easily than if you are in business as a sole trader.

Different ways to work and your rights

There are many different ways you can work. If you love your job, but just wish you had a bit more time with the family, why not ask to change your hours? If one of your children is under six, or you have a disabled child under the age of 18, or are a carer for someone who lives with you, you have the right to request this now, and there are proposals to extend these right to parents of older children too. Your employer does not have to change your hours, but does have to examine your request seriously.

You can ask:

- for a change to the hours you work, perhaps reducing the hours you do.

- for a change to the times you work. You may want to drop off the children at school or to pick them up.

- to work from home, all or part of the time.

 Heather has used the flexible working legislation to alter the hours she works as a computer programmer and computer support team leader. She says, "I had to apply to my employer in writing with my proposal and say what problems I thought this would give the company and how they could get around them. I knew I wanted to change my hours when my daughter started school so I gave about six months' notice – plenty of time to train someone else to provide cover." Heather now works from 7am to 2.30pm. She still puts in a 35-hour week but is always there to collect her daughter at the end of the school day. Her husband adjusted his hours slightly too, so he can do the school drop-off, and arrives at work for 9.30am. Heather goes on to say, "I love my new hours as I get to collect my daughter from school each day. My daughter gets some daddy time in the morning and mummy time at tea. Holidays are more of a challenge, with a mix of annual leave, grandparents and school club. My hours do mean that I can have a half-day of leave and in fact finish at 10.30, which means I only need someone to have her for a couple of hours."

Even if your children are older, it is still worth asking your employer for a change to your hours. There are lots of different ways to do a job, and you may want to suggest some of the ones below, or read about how other mums have done it:

Annualised hours

An annual number of hours are agreed, and you then work out with your employer when you will work. This could be something like two weeks on, two weeks off, or you may be able to work all your hours in term time.

Compressed hours

You still do the same hours, but over fewer days. This could mean doing four 10-hour days, or perhaps working a nine-day fortnight of nine-hour days.

 Matilda is a civil servant who currently works a nine-day fortnight. She's tried various different working patterns since she had her children, now five and three. Matilda says, "I went for a nine-day fortnight as a way to balance the need to earn money and continue my career with also having a little more time at home. I have to make the most of my day off, as there is never enough time to do everything. I'd always suggest to other parents to ask about flexible working – if you don't ask, you don't get. Because I have always been allowed hours which suit me, I am open to give back into my job when it's needed. But I do think it's important to stick to your overall hours: even if everyone else seems to work long hours it doesn't make it the best or only way."

Flexitime

This usually means that you work seven-and-a-half or eight hours between 7am and 7pm – a good arrangement for doing the school run at one end of the day or the other.

 Emily Williams has achieved a flexible mix of office and home based work since she returned to work after the birth of her second child. She now works as a project officer for the Kent and Medway Walking Bus Charity. Emily says, "I work ten hours in the office and then do the remaining six from home. I fit those hours in as and when I like during the week, and may work for part of the weekend or spread it over a few evenings. I take each holiday as it comes depending on my plans for work during that period. During the week, my six month old goes to a child minder for the hours I am in the office. As I can work flexibly it is not a problem if my baby, or the childminder, is ill. I just work from home. I can take the baby into the office for a short while to pick up papers. I adjust my hours to fit in with school events." Emily had to rearrange her working life to get to this stage. Before her second maternity leave she worked as an admin assistant 16 hours each week and did a few hours each week for the Walking Bus group. The admin job had limited prospects and was not as flexible, so she applied for the project officer position. She says, "I asked my boss if I could start slightly later each day to fit in with the hours that the childminder offers." Overall, Emily's current work pattern suits her down to the ground.

Homeworking

Could all or part of your job be done just as effectively from home? You will need to make sure you stay in touch with the office, and may need to attend meetings. Time you take off during the working day may need to be made up in the evening.

 David works part-time for a wildlife charity, with a mix of days at the office and at home. His partner does the same. He says, "My partner and I both enjoyed our nine to five jobs and wanted to continue with them, but we also both wanted to spend time at home with our daughter. We work at the same charity, so negotiated with our employer a flexible arrangement. Now we both work 25 hours a week with a mix of office and home working." David really enjoys his work-life balance and values spending time with his daughter while being able to keep his satisfying job. He comments, "I didn't want to see my family only at weekends, but at the same time I didn't want to throw in my career, and I have found a way of working which means that I don't have to do either of these things." It isn't always straightforward, and David has to slot work into evenings and weekends occasionally. He says, "Problems occur when our 18 month old daughter doesn't nap, or is teething, for instance. The hardest part is the 'tug-of-war' for my time. On the one hand I have an urgent email to answer but my daughter is tired and crying and needs changing. I can feel torn. It is possible to be a hard working professional and a good father, but it isn't easy to be both at the same time."

Job sharing

This is where you work with a partner, covering a single job, but splitting the days of the week between you. You will need good handovers, perhaps with a time where you are both in the office to discuss what is going on. It can be problematic to find the right job share partner.

Yvonne works as a legal secretary, and does a job share. Her work runs from 6.30pm to 2am, three nights a week. She says, "Because I do a job share I can swap the occasional night with my 'other half' which frees me up for school activities like parents evenings." Advantages for her include the ability to take her children to and from school, and participate in the school parents' forum. She continues, "I am here if the children want friends round after school. Now that I work part-time I have a few nights during the week where I get to cook for the children, bath them and get involved in bedtime." Yvonne's husband has flexible hours so can make sure he is home to do bed time on the nights she works. The main disadvantage for Yvonne? "Obviously it can be tiring because I get home at 3am and have to wake at 7am to get the girls to school. If I am tired I then go back to bed for a couple of hours." Yvonne's qualifications mean that she gets a good salary for her work. She says, "Some of my friends work evenings too, stacking shelves. I don't miss the nine to five and the rush hour and even during the school holidays I'm free to spend the day with the kids."

Self-rostering

This is where you select the hours to work that will suit you, and fit in with the needs of your employer.

Shift working

There are many jobs outside the traditional nine to five. Consider evening and weekend working and you may be able to arrange things so either you or your partner is always there for the kids

Staggered hours

Start and finish times can vary for different people in a team, so some finish early, while others start and finish late.

Term-time working

This works well if your company has seasonal demands, and is likely to be quiet during August, Christmas and Easter.

Parents of children under five are also entitled to 13 weeks' unpaid leave. There are proposals to extend this to other carers too.

Chapter 2

Hobbies into business

Wouldn't it be great to spend each day doing your favourite hobby and make money at it too? In this chapter we look at parents who have turned their hobbies into businesses, and how you can do it.

Having a passion is a key to success when you start a new business. Basing your business on a hobby you love can be a real winner. You get time to spend on your activity, improve your skills, get feedback from people who love what you make, and even earn money.

If you have been doing a hobby for years you may already have feedback from people who want to buy something from you. It isn't always straightforward to go from making something for fun to selling it for profit. There are regulations to follow, and you need to reach out to lots of potential customers to sell your items. Also, profits on handmade items can be low. Work out your prices carefully so you do not end up working for nothing. On balance, though, turning a hobby into a business can be a fulfilling way to earn pocket money and more, and it is a great way back to working. Read on to find lots of ideas for businesses based on hobbies.

Selling collectables

Whether you are an avid philatelist or have hundreds of Beanie Babies, there is an enormous market for selling collectables. If you collect something, the internet gives you massive scope for getting in touch with other people willing to part with cash for your finds. You will need to search constantly for more stock, but that is usually a pleasure rather than a pain for collectors. Getting the price right is harder – you need to buy bargains which you know will sell for more. From autographs and programmes to cigarette cards and phone cards there is a market for every collectable. Search **www.ebay.co.uk** on 'collectable' for around 50 more ideas of what sells. There are more specialist buying and selling websites such as **www.abebooks.co.uk** for books: you will probably know where you search for additions to your own collection. Check out the chapter on internet businesses for more on setting up your own online store.

Sue Sims has collected school stories all her adult life and says, "As with all collectors, I acquired duplicates as I upgraded or forgot I already had a particular school story. For several years I sold those duplicates to dealers. It struck me that I might sell them myself and take all the profit, so I advertised in Exchange & Mart, produced a short list, and that was the beginning." Sue combines bookselling with a career in teaching, and spends less time selling books when term is in full flow. She continues, "At the peak, I was spending an average of about 12 hours a week selling books. The work was actually concentrated into short bursts when a sales list went out, which I always did in the school holidays. Then I'd spend about 12 hours a day on it for around two to three weeks." Sue points out the downside of selling something you love to collect: "I don't really make much money, actually, as all the really good stuff goes straight into my collection, but the best thing is being able to buy books without feeling guilty. One also 'meets' a lot of other collectors via email, letter or phone." If you want to get started, Sue advises building up a mailing list of enthusiasts. After her initial ad she advertised in the *Book and Magazine Collector*. She concludes, "It's got hard to find stock now. I don't have much time. If you want to make a business out of collecting, I'd say either change from being mostly a collector to being mostly a dealer, or recognise that you'll never make much money."

Cooking

If you're hot in the kitchen there are lots of ideas for your own business. Before you get out the pans, register with your local authority. You will have to meet hygiene standards. Your local authority should be able to provide you with a 'food safety management pack', and will come round and inspect your premises periodically. See the Food Standards Agency booklet, 'Starting Up – Your First Steps to Running a Catering Business'. If you love to cook but are in need of inspiration, how about:

- Jams and pickles to sell at craft fairs or delicatessens

- Birthday cakes

- Catering for kids' parties

- Frozen home-cooked meals for new mums or time-poor business people

- Ethnic specialities

- Buffets and party platters of canapés

 Alexina Golding of Cakes2Party4 started her cake-making business after she enjoyed creating one for her daughter's first birthday. Alexina has converted a room in her house into a workspace. She says, "The room was originally the living room but we had an extension and then turned it into the playroom. When my son was due to start school we changed its purpose again as I had more time to develop the business." Alexina contacted the local environmental health department. Most of her plans were fine, although she had to add a sink with an extra half basin so there was a separate place for hand washing. Alexina says, "When it was completed they checked it out. The officer was impressed with the room. I even have the cutest handles in the shape of cakes, which does inspire my creativity." Alexina's room is off a small corridor so clients can enter without disturbing the home. Advantages for Alexina include having a place to see customers, and space to leave work out, to dry, which is vital for sugar flowers. She says, "Before I built my room I would have to tidy away the kitchen table and make sure that I wasn't using the oven for baking if I needed to make dinner. Now I have two double ovens in my room, and if pushed can use the one in the kitchen. I feel like I 'go to work', and can shut the door on everything at the end

> of the day. In the summer I can bake two three-tier wedding cakes at the same time. I can bake a fruit cake in one oven at a lower temp and a sponge in the other. I also offer cake stands for hire as there is now space."

Knitting and sewing

Having kids seems to bring out a creative streak in many people. If you love to knit or sew you may want to see if you can earn by selling your creations. Some mums start making clothes for their own kids, and get asked to make for others too. Check out the market, look at what similar items go for, and scope out where and how you would sell things.

Legal issues

There are regulations which you need to bear in mind when sewing and knitting. For example, pyjamas, baby's garments and cotton terry towelling bathrobes must meet flammability standards or be labelled 'keep away from fire'.

Pattern copyright

There are also legal issues surrounding the use of patterns. If you buy a pattern you usually just purchase the right to make the item for your own, or your family's, personal use. So, if you want to set up in business, check your patterns first. If you want to use someone else's pattern, you may need to buy a licence.

Cottage industry licences

A 'cottage industry licence' is a term more often heard in the US. It is an agreement whereby you pay a fee to allow you to use certain patterns to knit or sew for profit. This covers the pattern designer's development costs. You may be limited to the number of each item you can create, and these licences are not designed for big businesses, just for one or two people creating at home. To avoid copyright issues, design your own patterns. If you want to set up as a dressmaker, you can get the client to purchase a pattern instead, and then pay you to make the garment, which avoids any need for licences.

Fabric design rights

One further area to check is the designs on the actual fabric you use. Companies like Disney are incredibly protective of their rights, and will clamp down on small sellers offering, say, handmade Snow White bedding using Disney character fabric.

More ideas

If you don't want to create and sew garments, think about toys and dolls. Again, check the regulations with your local trading standards. Another sewing idea is to offer repairs and alterations. Many people without sewing skills or short on time would love to be able to drop items round to someone with a sewing machine for hemming and alteration. See if your local college has dressmaking courses if you need to develop your skills in this area, and look into insurance, just in case a repair goes wrong.

Cathie Chant has knitted since she was small. She runs Natural Knits for Nippers, selling knitted items including cloth nappy covers. She has developed her own knitting patterns too. To complement her own products she also sells fair trade clothing. She says, "I work in the morning and afternoon but down tools around four to make the evening meal for the children. Once they are tucked up in bed I usually put in another three to five hours. My hours of work vary considerably depending on the level of orders." Because of the variable level of orders, Cathie sometimes calls on her mum, who lives just round the corner, to help out with childcare. Not everyone has been so supportive, though. Cathie comments, "Close family and friends don't under-stand why I want to run my own business and have suggested I'd be better off with a 'proper' job. I am enthusiastic about what I do and enjoy it, and it means I can be on hand for my children." Other problems hindered Cathie when starting her business. She says, "It hasn't been easy to get finance for the business, and good quality suppliers have high minimum orders which can be a barrier to getting started. Others will only supply businesses that have premises." Cathy has plans to expand her business in the future and sell patterns and kits, but a lot of her plans are on hold until her daughter starts school.

Companies offering cottage industry licences:

- **www.littleturtleknits.com** adult and children's clothes and accessories

- **www.fernandfaerie.com** cloth nappy, baby carriers, rag dolls and more.

- **www.babybyyou.com** cloth nappy patterns

- **www.elizabethlee.com** maternity wear

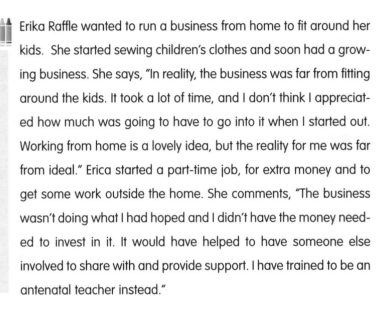

Erika Raffle wanted to run a business from home to fit around her kids. She started sewing children's clothes and soon had a growing business. She says, "In reality, the business was far from fitting around the kids. It took a lot of time, and I don't think I appreciated how much was going to have to go into it when I started out. Working from home is a lovely idea, but the reality for me was far from ideal." Erica started a part-time job, for extra money and to get some work outside the home. She comments, "The business wasn't doing what I had hoped and I didn't have the money needed to invest in it. It would have helped to have someone else involved to share with and provide support. I have trained to be an antenatal teacher instead."

Art, crafts and photography

If you love to paint or take photographs, it is encouraging to know that many mums, and dads, have made successful second careers out of their love of creative arts. Think about how your unique talents can best be used, and what you can offer that might be different or unusual, as this makes it easier to sell. Card making, for example, is an area with lots of competition, so look for a unique niche. Could you specialise in birth announcements, wedding or party invitations? Or, could your angle be the illustrations you create for the front of the cards? How about developing a line in business stationery? Get a good relationship with a local printer and see what other stationery services you could offer. Alternatively, focus the business on children. Look at the events children celebrate and offer kids' birthday cards, letters from Santa, or cards from the tooth fairy.

Why not look down the list, below, for inspiration, or read about three photography, painting and jewellery businesses:

Crafty business ideas

Painting	Making soap and other bath products
Pottery	Candle making
Photography	Woodwork
Jewellery making	Leatherwork
Selling craft supplies	Glass painting
Model making	Crochet
Tie-dyeing and batik	Soft toys or dolls' clothes
Embroidery	

 Christopher Perceval has a long-standing interest in photography, and took the decision to swap his legal career to work as a professional photographer. He says, "My wife works too, so having control over my own time means I can take our sons to school. It is hard work being your own boss. You also have to be the marketing person, admin assistant and tea boy. The list of extra roles could really go on for ages: accounts clerk, finance director, post room, secretary and telephonist."

Sue Cook has an inspiring story of moving from science and ad sales to a full-time career painting. The mother-of-two from Oxfordshire paints in her studio every morning while her daughter is at pre-school, and also works evenings and weekends creating beautiful flower paintings. Her unique angle is that she will create commissions to co-ordinate with your interior decorations. Sue started by selling a painting on eBay. With the encouragement of her husband and friends on an online parenting forum she built a website and found more and more people were interested. She advertises her services in a wedding magazine, has had newspaper and magazine coverage, and has won an international artists' competition.

Lucy McGowan enjoyed making jewellery as a hobby and found that after she took a course at the local college, family and friends bought more necklaces and bracelets. She decided to turn her hobby into a business and actively reach out to a wider range of people. She says, "My website, **www.chutneybeads.co.uk** has been key to this. I am creating a strong brand, which is as important as the product nowadays. Jewellery is a saturated market, and competition is my biggest problem. The branding helps with this, and I offer great customer service. I have also stuck at the types of jewellery I do best."

Jess Williams used to run a painted wooden products business. She says, "I really enjoyed doing this but the business was never very profitable. I also did some graphic design freelance work, and was trying to do too many things at once." In the next chapter you can read how Jess found her niche as a graphic designer.

Unusual hobbies

If you have a passion for something, there is usually a way to make it pay. Parents with unusual hobbies share how they did it, below:

 Barrie Clarke taught martial arts as a hobby for 15 years and eventually got frustrated with teaching in unsuitable halls. He decided to aim for his own martial arts academy, and has spent a couple of years getting this project off the ground. He focuses on free self defence classes for children, teaching them about stranger danger alongside fitness and martial arts. He says, "If you have an inspired idea, just go for it. You will feel better just doing something you really want to do. I'm happier and less stressed. This has a knock-on effect on the people around me, particularly my partner and children. I am now ready to franchise my business model so there are more dedicated academies like mine for children around the country."

Michelle Lawrie's interest in sign language has inspired her business idea. She took an evening class in British Sign Language (BSL), which came in useful when she worked at a day centre for adults with learning disabilities. She kept on studying until she gained her level three BSL qualification. Having heard that signing helped babies communicate, she also began to teach her children a few basic signs. She has now started an online store, **www.chelltune.co.uk**, selling baby sign language and BSL resources, which she combines with working as a communication support worker at a local college. She says, "I couldn't afford childcare for two pre-school children, so my work on the website fits in when it can. Any money we make from the website goes straight back into improving it at the moment."

Sally Akins used cloth nappies for her second son and found friends wanted her advice. She put information about nappies on a website, which turned into **www.treehuggermums.co.uk**, a resource for information about natural parenting. The website grew in popularity and in 2004 she started selling cloth nappies via the site. Sally says, "I had been a full-time working mum until my eldest son was three and a half and found it hard to juggle his needs with my career. Now I can pick the boys up from school and talk to them about what they have been doing." Sally's passion for green living makes running her website a pleasure. She enjoys picking products to sell that she would choose for her own family. Eventually she aims to offer family friendly employment to other parents.

Take action

Hopefully you now have more ideas of hobbies which could turn into good businesses. If you do start a business like this, make sure you still spend time enjoying yourself. Otherwise, you may find that you feel like you are working during all your spare time, and the hobby you once loved becomes 'work'. Find other things to do to switch off and wind down, and still spend some time just relaxing each evening.

If you don't feel inspired by making a product, read the next chapter to find out about a range of services that people offer from home or which can be offered with flexible hours.

Chapter 3

Services

Do you have a skill that might make a great business? This chapter looks at the sort of services that you can offer from home or with flexible working hours. And, if you don't have a skill already, there's information on retraining.

Therapist, doula, virtual assistant, web designer – there are lots of careers that can fit with your family. Some need nothing more than a desk. For others you have to go to clients' premises. Run through what you are looking for from a business so you can see if any of the ideas in this chapter suit you. Read the ideas section, then go on to find out more about the practicalities.

From pregnancy care to teaching

If having children has turned your life around, you might like to look at taking your interest in pregnancy, birth or childcare further.

Become a doula

A doula is a woman who supports mothers during and after birth. Courses cost from a few hundred pounds for a combination of weekend and home study. You need to be flexible if you want to be a birth doula, as births take place at all hours. If you want a career you can fit with school hours, some doulas just offer postnatal support, helping new mums with cooking, cleaning and washing as well as baby care. See the Doula UK website for more: **www.doula.org.uk**

Antenatal teaching and breastfeeding support

The NCT (National Childbirth Trust) offers training to become an antenatal teacher, Early Days facilitator or a breastfeeding counsellor. These university-accredited courses are part-time, with a mix of tutorials and distance learning. After completing the course the NCT expects you to work in your local NCT branch. Antenatal course teachers are in demand. There is an official rate of just under £9 an hour, but some areas pay more. Some teachers branch out to offer private courses too. Breastfeeding counsellors are usually volunteers, and can train through the Association of Breastfeeding Mothers and La Leche League as well as the NCT. Government programmes like Sure Start sometimes offer funding for breastfeeding sup-port workers.

Jean trained as an NCT antenatal teacher after her second baby was born. She says, "I attended a class during my first pregnancy and was inspired. It took until after my second baby was born for me to find time to train. I completed the training in just under three years, and managed to give birth to two more daughters too." Jean taught antenatal classes for her local NCT, together with a friend, Sam, but the women wanted more control over the class content. They saw that some areas were desperately short of antenatal teachers and spotted the opportunity to set up private classes.

Fitness fans

Other parents train as fitness instructors. Look for a course which enables you to join on the Register of Exercise Professionals. Courses are run by Central YMCA Qualifications, Active IQ and the Keep Fit Association. If you have a fitness qualification already, for a few hundred pounds you can take a specialist training course, like those offered by Buggyfit or the Guild of Pregnancy and Postnatal Exercise Instructors.

 Liz Stuart trained as a fitness instructor when working in IT. She says, "It was a volatile time and I wanted something to fall back on if redundancy struck." Liz's foresight paid off when she was made redundant a few months before she was due to give birth. She says, "It came together well. I wanted time with my new baby and I knew I had a plan for flexible work when I wanted to start again." Liz's career took a new twist when she started doing some informal exercise in the park with other friends who had babies of a similar age. She saw there was a need for exercise that new mums could do without having to find and pay for expensive childcare. Liz called her classes Power Pramming. She started charging, and the classes grew and grew. Liz now has another couple of instructors running classes across South London and plans for expansion.

Childcare careers

If you have thought about a career in childcare, you may want to check out your local Early Years unit, part of your local authority. They may offer courses to help you get started as a childminder, at little or no cost. These courses may have childcare provided, as many people wanting to work in childcare are parents already. If you complete the course, you may also get assistance with start-up costs, as part of government initiatives to increase the availability of childcare. Becoming a childminder allows you to stay home with your children, but think carefully about how you will manage if, for example, your child is sick.

Train to teach

Teaching is another career that you may want to investigate, not least because of the benefits of school holidays. There will always be a few days to cover, if you are called in for a staff training day, or if your children are sick.

 Vanessa Mitchell chose a teaching career as she wanted to be able to be financially independent but focused on her family. She says, "My job involves some flexibility in terms of more vacation time and fewer obligatory hours on site than most full-time jobs. It does not require fewer hours, but I have the flexibility of working at home or at school on the weekends or late at night. A teaching career has allowed for the flexibility I need to prioritise my family, but I had not foreseen the cost of childcare and the problems when my daughter is ill. On a teacher's salary, her day care is half my post-tax earnings. When she is ill I have to pay the nursery and pay our back-up person, or get docked my pay for taking a day off during term. Either way, it is twice the cost of her regular care."

Personal services

If you have an interest in complementary therapies or beauty there are many possibilities open to you. Most local colleges offer courses in a range of relevant subjects which could start you on the road to a new flexible career. Look at the length and structure of the courses. Some qualifications can be gained part-time or by attending weekend workshops over a period of months. It can take several years to train in therapies such as osteopathy, chiropractic or homeopathy.

Beauty and complementary therapies

Working as a beauty therapist or complementary therapist can fit well if you need a flexible career. You can offer your services at times that suit you, and some people convert a room in their home, which minimises travelling time. You need to work out childcare, as a relaxing massage would not be so relaxing if your toddler was playing in the corner of the room.

Beauty training

If you want to train, check out your local college. For Beauty Therapy an NVQ is a good grounding and can be taken part-time over a couple of years. ITEC diplomas are practically based and will provide you with the knowledge and skills you need to work in a range of beauty and complementary therapies such as massage, reflexology and aromatherapy.

Therapy training

The Research Council for Complementary Medicine lists universities offering a range of courses on their website, and also has details of the professional bodies for most of the complementary therapies listed below. The professional bodies can put you in touch with training colleges. Courses range from a few weeks to several years – watch out for short courses as they may not qualify you actually to practise safely on clients. Ask what you will be able to do at the end of the course as part of making sure the course is right for you.

 Morag Morrish says: "I worked in engineering and manufacturing, and took a part-time project manager position for the local council when Marlon was 18 months old. Although I enjoyed working there I wanted something more flexible to fit around school hours in preparation for my daughter starting school." Morag had practised yoga for seven years and felt becoming a yoga teacher would help her escape the constrictions of work. She explains, "Whilst on a training weekend, I met a colleague who had done YogaBugs training and was so enthusiastic about it that I contacted them straight away. It hadn't occurred to me to teach children. The minimum requirement to train with them was two years' continual yoga practice, which I had and so I could train, start teaching and earn an income straight away." Before Morag took the course, she thought ahead and wrote to her local schools before they broke up for summer to invite them to book a free taster session at the start of the September term. She now teaches six half-hour classes each week, including one at a private pre-school, and a lunchtime class at her daughter's school. She says, "For the hours that I can work, I earn enough money to contribute to the basic household costs whilst I build my reputation and take care of my children. The income also means I can sometimes put a little money aside to help contribute towards family holidays. The course cost £495 and I earned this back in the first six weeks of teaching. I'm now ready to put more hours in and have developed a plan so schools make YogaBugs part of their curriculum classes and I teach within school hours. Parents have asked me to take the Yoga'd Up course so that I can continue to teach their children as they reach eight. When my children become more independent, I will probably place the emphasis on adult teaching."

More ideas for therapies

Acupuncture	Homeopathy
Alexander Technique	Hypnosis
Aromatherapy	Iridology
Ayurvedic Medicine	Kinesiology
Bach Flower Remedies	Massage Therapy and Bodywork
Bowen Technique	Meditation
Chiropractic	Naturopathy
Colour Therapy	Osteopathy
Craniosacral Therapy	Reflexology
Crystal Therapy	Reiki
Feldenkrais Method	Shiatsu
Healing	Tai Chi
Herbal Medicine	Yoga

Other services

You will probably have seen people advertising as life coaches. This is a fast growing industry and offers the potential for working flexibly over the phone from your home. Life coaches help their clients work out and achieve goals in their career, relationships or pretty much any area of life. Life coaching isn't regulated in the UK, so anyone can call themselves a life coach. Check out courses carefully, and see what former students say about them.

Other personal services you could train to offer include colour analysis or wardrobe decluttering. Or, you may feel inspired by astrology or tarot readings. Learn Direct has lots of information and contacts if you want to find out more about many careers.

Domestic services

If you look after your own house, you probably have skills that people will pay for. Ironing and cleaning are a good start. Cleaning jobs can be on a self-employed basis, where you go to clients' homes, or you may find employment with a contract cleaning company. Work in clients' homes can fit between school runs, but may not be so easy to combine with toddlers. Contract cleaning often needs to be done at unsociable hours, so might be perfect if you can fit in a job in the early mornings, before offices open, or during the evenings. If you offer ironing, you will probably be able to do it from home. Find customers for cleaning and ironing by putting a notice in local shop windows.

Errand service

Could you wait in for deliveries or buy things for people who are too busy to get to the shops? If you have time on your hands but need money, link up with someone who is in the opposite situation and would gladly pay you by the hour to avoid taking time off work. Promote your services to local companies with high-flying executives and with postcards through the doors of expensive houses where the residents appear to be at work all day. One note of caution: if you have small children, think about how you would combine this with an active toddler. Waiting for deliveries in someone's home may be better if you have school-age children. You could still offer to drop off and collect dry cleaning, go to the post office and similar errands.

You can also work for courier companies, who pay by the item for deliveries. Read how one woman does this:

 Jane is mum to two teenagers and works as a secure document courier. She says, "I spend most of the day out on my bike, delivering items like new credit cards to people in the area I cover. I make an early start and collect the items to deliver that day at seven. This gives me a good chance of delivering most items, as I only get paid for successful deliveries." Jane works until around 5pm, but if you only have school hours available you can ask for a smaller area. The job is flexible, and Jane enjoys the outdoor work. She continues, "I like being constantly on the go, I can eat as much as I like and still stay slim as I ride my bike all day. On the downside, if I'm sick I don't get paid, and I have to cover the cost of repairs to my bike. I get to know people in the local area quite well, but it can be lonely too. And if my company loses a contract, my income falls as there are fewer items to deliver."

Richard Boyd walked away from his high pressure job running an IT and multimedia company after a breakdown. His wife suggested retraining, and he looked at property development, which would use his renovation skills. He decided that the market was saturated, so went for landscaping. He says, "I did not have the background knowledge needed. I had done our gardens but never got the look and feel that I wanted." He took a part-time job to pay the bills while he studied. He says, "When I completed my studies, I redesigned and landscaped two gardens. Neither was easy and I was hooked." Now Richard's business, Real Oasis, offers garden design and landscaping, events floristry, and topiary and exotic plants hire. He also runs some specialist horticultural online directories which bring in advertising revenue and keep his income flowing during the quieter winter months. Richard's enterprises now make up around half the family income. He says, "Starting up was difficult. It's competitive and there are a frightening number of contractors who do landscaping work without much horticultural knowledge. Finding good products and suppliers is always an issue. It can be hard to persuade clients that it is worth spending more on a better quality product which will last."

More domestic jobs

House finding	Ironing
Gardening	Driving/delivery/distribution
Childminding	Building flatpack furniture
Interior design	Cleaning
Decorating	Pet sitting
Decluttering	Dog walking
Party planner	Party organising
House cleaning	Wedding planning

Going freelance

If you have a skill that you have used in your career, could you do it freelance? Using a skill people know you have a talent for will help you when starting out. You should also look at people from previous employment and consider whether they could help you. Some may directly employ freelancers. If so, get in touch with a good résumé of your skills and experience. Even if they know you well, it won't hurt to remind them what you offer, and they may pass your details on. Even if you have contacts who don't directly employ freelancers, tell them you are looking for work and ask them to recommend you if colleagues need help.

Register with appropriate online freelance directories. **www.elance.com** is one of the biggest, but you have a lot of competition and may not get the best rates; **www. freelancers.net** is a UK based site with an IT focus. Research rates for your job. Your union cannot recommend a rate as this is illegal, but may have collected data on what members charge. Ask friendly colleagues for advice, or check out other people's websites if they display rates. **www. people4business.com** has a wide range of freelancers and displays their hourly rates.

Set up a website outlining what you offer, with up-to-date examples of your work. If someone wants to see what you do, referring them to your website is quicker than posting examples. Then, if they need someone urgently they can make a swift decision and you will have an advantage over freelancers who have to send examples of their work and experience by mail.

 Helen used to work in publishing and now offers proof-reading, copy editing and research from home. She says, "When I handed my notice in after having my first child I resigned and asked for freelance work all in the same breath." She enjoys the flexibility of working while the children are napping or at school. However, going freelance was not easy. Helen says, "Early on I had to pluck up the courage to cold-call potential clients. It was worth making myself do it though as it led to the regular clients I still have now. I haven't had to look for work in quite a while, it tends to find me." Another problem can be taking on too much at once. Helen comments, "It is hard to say no when you're not sure where the next job is coming from. I have three or four regular clients and a much clearer idea of when work will come in. It can be hard to switch off when you know that the work is there. Once the children are in bed I sit straight down and some nights I need to work until midnight or later, which can be exhausting." Helen beats stress by making firm plans for one night each week, either getting a babysitter and going out with her partner or getting a bottle of wine in. She adds, "I'm considering getting a childminder one day a week for my youngest, to enable me to get more done in the day and free up some evenings. Overall, though, I feel privileged to be able to spend so much time with my children while still earning a living."

More ideas for freelance services

Writing	Translation
Graphic design	Marketing
Human resources	Event management
Programming	Research
CV writing	Project management

 Kamaljeet was no longer prepared to spend 14 hours a day at work, so he took redundancy when it was offered. He uses the skills he developed throughout his employed career, to offer management consultancy in change management and equality. His hours are flexible and he sees more of his children, spending at least a couple of days each week at home. He says, "It's great not to be drowning in emails or involved in petty office politics. It's harder to keep focused and my day can easily be taken over by the kids." If you are thinking of becoming a freelance consultant, Kamaljeet says, "Keep your focus. You need to motivate yourself. Be resilient, and prepare for periods of famine and feast. Sometimes you can be working all the hours available, and other times you spend every day with the family."

Patricia Saing wanted more control over her life, after a career in further education, and decided tutoring could be the answer. She works flexible hours tutoring students online and at home in biology and animal management. She says, "I work when I want, and I have done things I never thought I would do, such as setting up lab facilities for an academic institution; being involved with child protection; teaching IT and working at a zoo. You need to work out how to manage with less money and stick at promoting your services, but I'd tell anyone thinking of working more flexibly to be brave and go for it."

Jess Williams offers graphic design and illustration services from home. She started Greensand Design when her daughter was six months. She says, "To start with I worked while she napped, and as she got older she played beside me, or I would work when my husband could care for her. This meant a lot of evening and weekend working. I have never needed to pay for childcare although I have had to call on friends and family now and then when a deadline is looming." Now her daughter has started school Jess is able to develop her business. She says, "I finally have the time available to use resources like Business Link, something I have wanted to do for the last five years." Jess concludes, "Much like having children, the bad bits of working for yourself are much worse than you imagine, but the good bits are so much better."

Euan Stuart had always wanted to write, so after his daughter was born he changed career. He ditched his job in the city to combine writing with being a stay-at-home dad. Euan says, "Make sure you have some work organised before changing career. It is hard to earn a good wage in this way. The main benefit for me is being able to spend time with my daughter, and to some extent my wife. Lack of stress and better personal health are other satellite benefits."

Admin support

This is a freelance service which merits its own section because it is one area where anyone with a computer and reasonable language and IT skills can start a business. Play to your strengths. If you are good on the phone, some businesses may need people to make sales calls for them. Others may want a 'virtual receptionist' to answer the phones. This is not ideal if you have noisy children at home, but may work well if your children are at school. Lots of companies outsource data entry. You could contact local firms or advertise at colleges to see if anyone needs typing or transcription. This sort of work could be fitted in during the evenings and nap times.

Other services you could offer include all sorts of admin tasks, writing letters, creating databases and spreadsheets or doing PowerPoint presentations. Companies such as local estate agents may need help with mailshots. If you were already a secretary in your previous career you have an advantage, of course, and legal or medical secretaries can find specialist work.

Think about the other skills you could combine with virtual admin support. If you have experience of writing, could you offer editing and writing services? If you have a talent for computer graphics, how about specialising in desktop publishing? Or if you have a good head for figures, why not focus on bookkeeping? A short evening course can help you get your specialist skills up to scratch, and gives your admin business a unique angle to hook customers and keep them coming back to you.

Karen worked for Westland Helicopters before she had children. She says, "I worked as a programmer on the company intranet, writing code to connect the web pages to databases and managing the company internet service. Once I was pregnant with my second child, I didn't want to have to work the hours my employer would have liked, so I started my own business as a virtual assistant." Karen's IT skills came in useful, and she now offers web design for business clients.

Linda Baldwin took voluntary redundancy, and was looking for work when she saw an ad for a part-time home-based researcher for a headhunting company. After a few months as an employee, she moved into freelance recruitment, CV writing and telemarketing. She says, "I enjoy not having to commute, and working in comfortable clothes. I worked through my pregnancy and could lie down whenever I wanted. I worked with my baby at home for the first year, but then got a nursery place for him. I love working flexible hours and taking time off when I need." A couple of times Linda has been caught in the trap of relying on one company for the bulk of her work. She says, "I am now clear with clients that I only offer part-time services, so I can keep several firms on the go. It is hard to say no to work so sometimes I over-stretch myself." Linda comments that home-based work isn't for everyone as it can be lonely, but adds "I love writing away at my computer with Radio 4 to keep me company. I can take the dogs for a quick run and take my son to school too. Tell friends and family that you are working, as other mums may drop in for cof-fee and not understand that you have work to do. Train them to book a good time to meet rather than just dropping in."

Angela Ireland does flexible telemarketing work to fit in with school hours and the needs of her daughters. She says, "I want-ed to return to paid work, but as I have a child with cerebral palsy, I realised that no employer would grant me the amount of leave I would need for hospital appointments and sickness." Angela leaves enough slack in her work that she has time to catch up without clients suffering if she has to deal with a home emer-gency. She goes on to say, "I have no sickness cover for me, so I don't get sick often." She recommends that parents thinking of starting freelance work should be careful not to over commit, an easy trap to fall into when developing a freelance career.

Claire Dovey spent hours deliberating whether or not to return to work as a personal assistant after the birth of her son, Henry. Instead, she set up as a virtual secretary. She says, "During my first year I found more companies needed a virtual assistant than I had first thought. I now work full–time." Claire then had an idea to expand her business. She says, "I offer other people the oppor-tunity to work from home as virtual secretaries for their area. In return for a small start-up fee, VSS provides you with the tools to start working from home. You get your own business based around your area, a website page on the VSS website, an email address, a start-up pack containing all the forms and paperwork needed in dealing with clients, including terms and conditions."

Vicki Hill used her teaching skills to set up a company selling children's reward boards. She says, "I trained in children's behaviour and I recognised it was what parents had a problem with. There was a gap in the market at the time. I'd made charts for my son Joe and realised other parents needed them too." Vicki has now sold her business and gone back into employment. She says, "It was a good job for me at the time but the business grew to a stage where it needed me to invest heavily in it. As I was going through a divorce I wasn't able to take the financial risk associated with this. I reviewed the situation and although the business did pay, I felt that it wasn't worth working on every night for a small financial gain. It was a hard decision to sell the business although an excellent learning experience."

Mystery shopping

One more opportunity is to become a market researcher for a mystery shopping company. You are self-employed and the amount of work you get depends on your motivation and the amount of work each company has on. You can register with several at a time. You won't make a fortune doing this, but will earn a few quid an hour, get travel expenses, and may enjoy some free meals. You may be asked to check certain details with a shop or order something in particular, and you have to report on your findings. You need to have a reasonable memory. You may need a computer, as requests for shoppers are often sent out by email, and the first people to reply get the jobs. Your computer will also be needed so you can download and send reports. Not every opportunity is suitable if you have children with you.

 Sarah has four small children and does mystery shopping for a couple of companies. She says, "I pick and choose the assignments I want. Most of them are local to me. Occasionally I pick one further afield for a day out. The good thing is that the children can often come with me. You have to be prepared to put the time in and note all the details then fill in the questionnaires after, though, which can be time–consuming."

Finding clients

For any of these self-employed services, you will need to generate your own clients and the success of your business will depend on you getting people to pay for your services.

 Mark Lister retrained as a coach after a career in music. He says, "I went back to university at the age of 34 to study history, but there is a surplus of both musicians and historians. I found out a bit about self development and coaching, saw how it worked for me, and decided to retrain, which took about six months. The course ran over five three-day weekends, with lots of work in between. It was all practical and definitely helped me start to build my practice." Mark has one son and shares childcare with his ex. He says, "I negotiated childcare so I could retrain, and now what

I do is flexible. I manage my time so I can go on holiday with my son. I do most of my work during the daytime, with occasional evening clients. I sometimes do 12-hour days, but can take off for a bike ride on other days which compensates." It has taken a couple of years for Mark to build up the income from his coaching practice. He says, "I advertised in a range of magazines, some of which worked well. I now focus my coaching on men and fathers, and have found they tend to find me through the Yellow Pages rather than in magazines." Mark has some advice for anyone thinking of retraining: "A course will give you a set of skills, but it won't give you a business. Lots of people train as coaches, but don't get beyond seeing a few clients. Make sure you think about what you need to develop a business as well as professional skills."

Pricing your services

Everyone who offers a service has to decide on fees. This can seem harder than selling a product. Just how do you work out the right rate for your time? Start by looking at the competition. How much do other companies or individuals charge for similar services? You may start by charging one amount when you have little experience, then put your fees up as you get busier. Read how one businessmum did it:

Sadie Knight runs Glassraven Web Design. She says, "Pricing my services has got to be the hardest thing that I have had to do in my business life. You are not selling a solid item; you are selling skills and time. Looking at the competition you can see the huge variation in prices. A five-page website ranges from a few pounds up to a few thousand pounds for something that superficially looks the same, but with messy code and outdated design which can impact on a website's ranking. I made the decision to price myself affordably but not at rock bottom. I factored in that I enjoy working with small businesses. Seeing a company you work with growing from start-up to successfully established business is a fantastic feeling. I worked through how many projects I could do per month and then split the cost into what I needed to earn to cover my costs and earn a wage. I factored in time for maintenance of my websites and business administration.."

How to get help to retrain

This section looks at help with the costs of training and childcare for while you are studying.

Career Development Loan

If you need financial help to study, you can apply for a Career Development Loan. This is a deferred repayment bank loan to help pay for vocational learning or education. Anyone aged 18 or over can apply for the loan, to fund any full-time, part-time or distance learning courses of up to two years. If your chosen course is longer than two years you can use a CDL to fund part of it. You can borrow between £300 and £8,000. CDLs are available through three high street banks: Barclays, The Co-operative and The Royal Bank of Scotland. You do not need to be an existing account holder but the bank may want you to open one. The Learning Skills Council pays the interest on your loan while you're learning. You then repay it over an agreed period at a fixed rate of interest. The Career Development Loan website tells you how to apply.

Free childcare places

Children aged three and four are entitled to free part-time childcare, although the standard two and a half hours a day will probably only cover part of what you need. Places can be in school nursery or reception classes, day nurseries, play-groups or with some childminders. Contact your local Children's Information Service via ChildcareLink to find out about this. Young parents under 19 going back into learning get more help with childcare – several thousand pounds per child per year. Find out more by going to the Department for Education and Skills' 'Care to Learn' website.

Child tax credit

Child tax credit is based on your income, whether you are working or not. Contact the Inland Revenue to calculate how much you would qualify for and apply.

Access and hardship funds

Many colleges have a fund to help students in financial diffi-culties. They can be used for childcare, books, travel and equipment. They are usually one-off payments that you don't have to repay. Ask your college welfare office.

 Alison works in communications and is doing a two-year part-time course in silversmithing. She started making cards and jewellery while on maternity leave and built up a small business. Alison says, "I found the jewellery making fascinating and wanted to do more. I've now put the business on hold while I train and improve my jewellery making skills. My part-time job takes the pressure off financially while giving me time to train and develop the skills I need." There are downsides to having a job and a course on the go at the same time. Alison continues, "It is difficult if there is a work event on the day of my course. I have to make up time and find out what has been taught that day. And one day I had to leave the course early because my son's nursery called and said that their heating had broken and they were closing. The course has lots of extra costs too, such as workshop fees, buying tools, silver, books and stationery. Overall, though, I love it and can't wait to be a trained silversmith."

Chapter 4

Products

Many parents develop ingenious inventions. Some are inspired by a problem they have needed to solve themselves. Others get creative while appearing to be engaged with the children. It can be amazing what your brain comes up with while serving dinner or at bath time. This chapter tells you about how mums and dads got inspired, and the steps they took to get their idea on the market.

Having the idea

If you would love to come up with an idea for your own product, this is one area where there is no straightforward solution. You just need inspiration to strike. Try looking at problems which need solving. It may be easiest if you start thinking about an issue you are familiar with. Talk to other people about how they solve the problem, and read up about the subject. You might be inspired when you read on to find out how other parents have got their businesses going.

 Like many mums, Laura Park's business inspiration came from her solution to a problem. Her son cried 12 hours a day and hated being put down. She bought a sling and found he was far happier in it, but the sling was bulky and tricky to use. She searched online for something simple, but couldn't find what she wanted, so bought some fleece and experimented. Once she had perfected her design for a pouch sling and found it worked like a dream on her own baby, Laura was surprised to find friends wanting them too. She says, "I mentioned it on a parenting forum and got three requests. Soon I was getting half a dozen orders a week, so I set up a small online shop." Laura now offers her slings through retailers and **www.brightsparkslings.co.uk**.

Amy Warburton was forced to take things slowly due to illness. While she was stuck in bed and husband Paul did much of the childcare, Amy had some ideas. She says, "I read a lot while I was ill, and found out more about herbalism and aromatherapy. I'd always loved creative things and used a lot of candles, but hated the fact that they were all paraffin based. A few years back it was difficult to get beeswax or soy candles, so I spotted a niche in the market. I combined my knowledge and skills and started making beeswax candles."

Jon and Dan Brousson run Onya Bags. The bag was invented by Jon, who says, "Having known since the mid '80s that plastic bags are incredibly convenient, but terrible for the environment, I was troubled every time I forgot to take my reusable bags to the shops. One night whilst lying in a hammock gazing up at the stars I put some thought to this problem. A brilliant solution would need to be with you for every shopping trip, for all those unplanned 'spur of the moment' trips; as convenient as a plastic bag and certainly not bulky to carry around. Soon I was close to the answer; in fact I had been sitting on it for the past five minutes. My hammock was made from strong parachute material, had great colour and simply stuffed away into its own convenient pouch. Brilliant! These are the perfect principles for the bag we all need. I just needed to make sure it would never be forgotten, so I pondered, could a bag also fit on my front door key?" Jon now sells the bags across Australia, and Dan is responsible for UK sales.

Protecting your idea

Some products are made by many different companies. Each business needs to find a unique twist, like Amy's natural candles, and then sell to the right market. If you copy another company's idea you run the risk of legal action, as it may have protected the products and concepts.

Alternatively, you may think you have come up with a new idea for a product or service. If so, you will probably want to protect your idea. You can also protect the name and logo of your company. Read on to find out how, and what sort of protection is appropriate for your circumstances.

Copyright

Copyright protects written material, written and recorded music, and sound and visual recordings such as films. Copyright is automatically yours. Just keep copies of drafts and notes to show you are the originator of the material. You can send yourself a special delivery envelope containing your notes, which is one way to demonstrate a date of creation. There are also agencies which offer copyright registration for a fee. These are unofficial bodies. Check out what they offer for the fee, as you may get little benefit.

Designs

Designs lay out how products look. Like copyright, you get automatic 'design right' to something you have invented. Again, keep copies of the first notes you make and the first items you create. Your design is protected for 15 years after you create the design, or, if you put the product on sale, for ten years after the first sale.

You can register a design with the UK Intellectual Property Office within the first year of putting it in the public domain, which costs in the region of £60. Your design can be protected for up to 25 years, renewable every five years. You need to check that your idea hasn't been thought of before. To find out, browse catalogues, search on the internet, and look through designs registered with the UK Intellectual Property Office, (formerly the Patents Office). Then go on to fill in the forms you find on the UKIPO website: **www.ipo.gov.uk**.

 Bex Smith has created a number of baby products. She says, "I designed a cloth nappy system. It took me two and a half years of product development before I had a final design that I was happy to register. I went through plenty of prototypes and many different ways of doing things to find what worked best. This experience was useful when I came up with the idea for a baby change mat which you can popper over your baby's legs like a loose nappy to prevent 'wee' accidents. I got the initial design together within a week, and went through the design registration application a few weeks later." Bex found the process straightforward. "Registering the designs was easy. The forms are simple enough to do yourself. You can check through the registered designs database on the UKIPO website to ensure you are not doing something that has been done before. I have found that my initial investment of £60 has actually made my whole product range more valuable than it would have been."

Elizabeth Geldart of **www.chiggs.co.uk** has created a couple of handy products for parents. The Baby Feed Wheel is a simple card with a dial to record the time of your new baby's last feed. Elizabeth says, "When I first thought of the idea I couldn't believe that somebody hadn't already thought of it. I spent a couple of weeks trawling the internet for anything similar. When my research discovered nothing, I contacted the Patent Office [UKIPO]. Initially, I found the website rather confusing, but I phoned them up and found everyone I spoke to helpful, with good advice. I was told that as the 'dial' part of the card was already patented I could only register the design. In a way this was a good thing, as it saved money. When I described my product, the man at UKIPO said 'I don't think we have a category for this'. That's when I knew the idea was unique." After speaking to UKIPO, Elizabeth filed her application for a design patent. She didn't have a finished product, so made a prototype of the design and used images of that to form the basis of the application. She continues, "Once the application was approved and I received the Certificate of Design Patent, I had the Reg. Des. (registered design) number printed on the reverse of the Baby Feed Wheel. A few months later, I came up with the idea for the Baby Medicine Wheel, and repeated the process."

Patents

According to the UKIPO, patents protect the technical and functional aspects of products and processes. If you are thinking of applying for a patent, make sure your creation is new and inventive. There should not be anything like it already available. Be careful about discussing your idea. If you want to run it by friends or experts, get them to sign an agreement that they will keep your information under wraps. This is known as a non-disclosure agreement. Look at what else is available on the market and think about who might buy your item to make sure it is commercially viable before investing your time and money.

Patent searches and costs

There is a free online search of registered patents at **http:// gb.espacenet.com**. It costs an initial £30 to apply, there is a fee of £100 for the UKIPO to search to ensure your design is unique, and then you pay a further £75 for them to examine your application. The process takes at least two years. You need to have a description of your product, drawings, claims for what it does, and a technical summary in order to fill in the initial application forms on the UKIPO site. You may incur further costs during the process getting your product information and prototypes up to standard. You may want the help of a patent agent to get the application wording watertight.

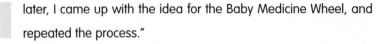

Patent protection

A patent protects your creation for up to 20 years, but you need to renew it in its fifth year and annually after that. You should also think about whether you want to apply for protection for your invention overseas. Some countries allow you to extend your UK patent, others have treaties on patents under which you apply, or you may have to apply to patent offices in individual countries.

Trade marks

If you have a logo, words or images which make your products and services stand out from those of another company, you have something which can be trademarked. It can't be similar to trademarks already registered for businesses in similar sectors. It costs £200 to register for one class of goods or services, plus an additional £50 for each further sector. There are 34 classes of goods and a further 11 classes for services. As an example, Class 25 includes clothing, footwear, and headgear. It is not compulsory to register a trademark, but it gives you protection for your brand.

Trade mark professionals

Trade mark attorneys and patent agents offer advice and can handle IP applications for you. Find an attorney through the Institute of Trade Mark Attorneys or the Chartered Institute of Patent Agents.

 Lou Simpson of Snugglytots has trademarked her company name and logo. She says, "The Welsh Development Agency paid half the fees, which made it more attractive. I paid for a search first, which was about £70 to check that my logo and name didn't clash with anyone else's, which was well worth it. If you apply for a trademark it costs £200 and if yours is similar to someone else's you won't get your money back. The forms look scarier than they are. They could make it a bit easier, but they were only at the end of a phone if I got stuck."

When Bonita of Twins Things applied to register her trademark, she had to register in 10 categories because of the wide range of products her company offers. She says, "I had the search done first to reduce the risk of the application failing and losing all the money. I used an agent to do my application, so she did all the legwork for me."

Liz Stuart of Power Pramming says, "I'm not the only person running this sort of exercise class. I have applied to register my trademark, but fear that the fact that people are beginning to use Power Pramming as a generic name for this sort of exercise class may be a problem. Competitors have even used it on their websites so people searching for my classes find theirs."

Nadine Lewis had started a home business as a virtual assistant when she was inspired to come up with a new product by a friend's car crash. Nadine says, "I was concerned about who would look after the children if I was unconscious after a car crash. Then something clicked. I realised how simple it would be to create a child ID card to attach to the side of a car seat, containing emergency contact information." Since that first idea, Nadine has created a range of ID products. She has trademarked her main brands, IdentiKids, IdentifyMe, and WickID, although her experience was far from straightforward. She says, "We filled in the forms and didn't expect any problems, but an objection was raised. It dragged out the process for several years and increased my costs significantly. Building a strong brand is vitally important, and the trademark is an integral part of this, so we had to invest time and money in registering and protecting it."

Intellectual property and paying yourself

One further benefit of registering a design, creating music or writing something, is that you are able to receive royalty payments on each item sold. This can have benefits in ensuring that you get a flow of payment as the money comes into your business, and can help you qualify for schedule D, or self-employed, status, for tax. This is particularly useful for home-based business, as you can count a proportion of your household costs against your business income. Check with an accountant how this will apply to your situation.

Regulations and testing

Depending on what you are making, your product may need to be tested or examined. Trading Standards offers information on regulations in areas such as labelling of textiles, cosmetic products, and the safety of consumer goods. Talk to the British Standards Institute to find out what standards might apply. They also offer product testing. Look at competitors to see if they make claims that their products live up to certain standards, and check whether these are mandatory or just good for marketing. You may want to mark your product with the CE mark, which indicates it complies with relevant European directives and aims to facilitate European sales.

Manufacturing your invention

Once you have thought about protecting your product, you need to get it made. It may be something you can make yourself. This is a low-risk way to build up your business gradually. Once your business grows, you may want to recruit outworkers.

Outworkers

Outworkers are usually self-employed and often work on a 'piecework' basis, where you pay them for each item they make, or by the hour. You need to have a contract with each outworker and provide clear information about the standards you expect. Outworkers are usually self-employed. Set up a simple form for them to complete stating how many items they have made. Then get them to invoice you for the amount you owe them. You inspect their work and then pay. You can supply work to the outworkers as and when you have it. They can be a valuable way to extend your capacity if you have a seasonal business. The National Group on Homeworking has resources and example terms and conditions for outworkers: **www.homeworking.gn.apc.org.**

 Lou Simpson got sewing when she bought a cosytoes for her new baby and found that it was too short and the fabric was too thin.

She says, "I made one from an offcut of fleece to go with his new buggy. Then a friend asked if I'd make her one, so I bought a few more metres and had enough left over for a second, which I put on eBay. Another friend asked me to make a navy cosytoes to match her buggy, and really encouraged me to offer the cosytoes for sale more widely. The unique angle for my business is that you could choose a custom fabric combination. I put a few auctions up on eBay for 'custom cosytoes' and it just took off. I took payment by PayPal and Nochex. Six years down the line, I sell cosytoes and buggy liners direct to consumers and wholesale. Because my products are seasonal, I use outworkers for sewing at busy periods, but finding reliable people of the standard I require hasn't been easy."

Manufacturers

If your item cannot be made at home, you will need to find a manufacturer. This can take considerable research, ingenuity and negotiation. Start by talking to your local enterprise agency. Look in local directories for manufacturing companies near you, as that can cut delivery costs. Search online for factories making products from materials similar to what you want. Online resources such as **www.alibaba.com** can put you in touch with companies overseas.

Elizabeth Geldart found the manufacturer for her Baby Feed Wheel by taking apart the car parking disc which had inspired her. The manufacturer's details were inside. "So," she says, "I got in touch and asked them to produce some in pink, blue and yellow. They were taken aback but managed it. I ordered 1,500 in the first place and customised them myself. My next order was for 5,000. Now I'm hoping to increase wholesale sales by continuing to add stockists, and increase my range of products."

Bex Smith says, "Finding manufacturing has not been easy. Factories don't like small runs. They need a good throughput to justify setting up the machines. I used a factory for a while, but the arrangement did not work so well after we moved house and delivery costs increased. I was less able to check on progress and chase up work. Instead I have bought the machines I needed to set up a workshop to get things made in-house, using self-employed outworkers when there is more work than I can manage."

Nadine Lewis of IdentifyMe has created a range of products. When developing the latest one, she says, "Firstly, we had to decide whether to manufacture the wristband in-house. We decided we didn't have the expertise, and the cost for the machinery was prohibitive. We looked at several manufacturers and found one that offered something we could work with. We took their basic design and spent several months in discussion, developing new moulds and new fastenings for the wristbands." Nadine has arranged a contract with the manufacturer to ensure that the product they have created is exclusive to IdentifyMe.

Jon Brousson has arranged the manufacturing for Onya Bags. Being based in Australia, he has been able to visit the factories they have used in Indonesia and China. Dan says, "Jon checked the working conditions and wages at both factories. The first was a family-owned business, but they weren't always able to meet our deadlines. We had a problem with an order that was delayed as they didn't work on certain religious days. We still use them for some things but the factory in China has a larger capacity. It is in a big university town and most of the work seems to be done by mature students working their way through their studies." Jon and Dan used the Australian trade commission, Austrade, to help them source the factory in China. UK Trade and Commission does a similar job.

Wholesaling

Once you have plans for product manufacturing in place, how will you sell your product? You may want to set up your own website or store and sell direct to consumers, but most people also end up selling an invention wholesale. The advantages are that you can shift larger volumes, and distribution costs come down if you send several hundred or several thousand products to one destination. Think about the packaging for each item, and how to distribute large quantities without the products getting damaged.

Wholesale buyers

Start by working out which retailers might sell your product. Draw up a target list. Think how you will present your product to them in a persuasive way. You need samples in professional packaging, promotional materials, and a list of reasons why the shop will be able to sell your items. Include favourable reviews, press cuttings and customer comments if you have them. Mention if you have advertising and PR planned. Think carefully about how much to charge for wholesale orders. Retailers will mark up the price you charge by 30 to 50 percent, and the more profit they can make, the more likely they are to consider stocking your item. The more you discount the wholesale price, the less profit you make yourself. Why not work out a sliding scale of discounts depending on order size? These, and other factors such as delivery terms, should all be part of your wholesale terms and conditions.

Start to sell

Once you have your wholesale information ready, pick a few smaller retailers to try it out on. Find out who is responsible for buying your sort of product. Larger companies have different buyers for different departments or categories. Each buyer may only look for new products at certain times of the year, and there is no guarantee that they want to widen their product range in your product area. Big retailers have forms and regulations that they will want you to comply with, if they want to buy your product. These can detail when they want the product, and how they want it packaged, marketed and delivered.

Dan approached a few shops, and says, "I didn't know what I was doing, and got turned down by the first three. Then, I was in an organic deli in Somerset. I had my bag with me as usual, and just thought I'd ask if they would consider stocking them. I was pleased when they did. The bags sold well, and the shop paid me promptly too, which spurred me on. I carried on taking the products to local shops, and found more store owners contacting me.

My bags have a visible logo and customers using them work as a great advertisement." Attending a trade show gave Dan a breakthrough. He says, "I went to Top Drawer Autumn. I was fortunate that it had an eco-friendly theme, and I was a featured seller. I got 62 trade orders during the show. People are still getting in touch. I have since done two more shows, with continuing success. Shows really seem to have a long term effect." In the last year, Dan estimates his turnover has increased to around £250,000, and Onya bags are now available in around 100 shops.

National accounts

Aiming for national accounts is not for everyone. There are downsides to supplying wholesale, and profits can get eaten away by retailers keen to extract the maximum discount.

Michaela from Nappies by Minki says, "At first I thought it would be great to see my products in Mothercare, but now I avoid large national accounts. My business is more secure relying on lots of small accounts than one or two big ones. I've looked at the margins too. We spread our wholesale business across Australia, New Zealand, Japan, the Netherlands, Germany and France as well as the UK. I get better returns by supplying medium-sized retailers and direct to the consumer."

Nadine Lewis started her business in a small way, selling direct to customers, but she now deals with buyers from major chains. She says, "Selling to big retailers is a complex business. Allow for it to take two years or more from approaching the company to seeing your products on the shelves. Buyers may not respond to your ini-

tial approach, and then out of the blue you will get a call, promoting a flurry of activity. You need to meet their requirements, fill
in their forms, and they will ask for discounts for payment on time
and even a contribution towards their advertising costs."

Chapter 5

Direct selling and party plans

Not everyone wants to invent their own product. This chapter looks at what's on offer if you want a business that is set up for you with low start-up costs up to a couple of hundred pounds.

Tupperware parties are legendary, and Avon ladies are seen in every town. You will probably know someone who is a rep for a direct selling company: there are over half a million people doing this in the UK. There are many different companies offering you the chance to sell their products direct to friends, relations and friends of friends, offering everything from baby wear to tools.

Becoming a rep is a good opportunity if you are looking for work to fit with the family, but you should enter into it with your eyes open. The clue to success for any direct selling opportunity is in the word 'selling'. You need to be prepared to twist arms, turn acquaintances into customers, and make the most of every occasion to sell.

What not to do

Watch out for scams. Later in the chapter, there are details of reputable companies with a track record who offer you a proper starter kit for your initial investment. There are always schemes to avoid. Steer clear of anything where it isn't obvious what you will sell. If you have to send £10 in response to an ad for homeworking opportunities, you may find they just suggest you place a similar ad and ask people to send money to you. This, in one form or another, is the basis for many scams.

Assembly scams

Envelope stuffing and other assembly schemes are often a front for scams too. Beware if you have to send a payment for the materials you are to assemble. You may well find that however hard you practise the company refuses to pay you as your efforts are substandard, or just doesn't get back in touch at all. Steer clear of opportunities that promise large rewards for little effort, or only offer contact through a PO Box or mobile number. Read the Office of Fair Trading website for more information on scams to avoid: **www.oft.gov.uk**.

Why not to become a rep?

It cannot be stated often enough. Becoming a rep requires hard work. You need to get a buzz out of selling to succeed. Weigh up how much spare time you have, and what part of that you can commit to delivering catalogues and orders, collecting and chasing payment, and promoting and planning parties. Additionally, you need to look at where your profits will come from, as you may make more money from recruiting new reps than selling products. In a survey, reps spent less than half their time selling, nearly one hour in five being on admin, and one in six on recruiting.

 Rebecca bought a Bioflow distributorship when she was made redundant from a warehouse job. She says, "I got up to exec level, but my heart wasn't in it. I am no salesperson. When push comes to shove more people buy if I pass them on to my brother, who is also a distributor, than I ever sold for myself."

Long term gains

There is a high turnover in direct selling organisations, with more than half of all reps selling for less than two years. Only a small percentage finds long term success. Direct selling is usually commission based, so there's no regular income, and you have to feel confident about getting people to buy. On the positive side, though, you're usually selling something with a bit of fun included, and you can arrange to work at times to suit you.

How to choose

Take a businesslike approach to working out what sort of opportunity would be right for you. Work out how much time you could spend promoting your products, and how this would fit with the children. Do you want to sell door-to-door, to local groups or at parties? Do you have a car to help you transport large boxes of samples? Some jobs will also require you to deliver customers' orders. Find out if you will need to store large amounts of stock.

Love what you sell

Make sure you are genuinely interested in and like the products. It is hard to sell something you would not use yourself. And think whether what you sell will interest people in your area. Check if you can buy the same thing in your local shops more cheaply. Are customers likely to return to buy their favourite products again and again, or are purchases likely to be a one-off?

SLM or MLM

Some companies give you just the opportunity to sell, person to person or by party plan. This is called Single Level Marketing (SLM). Part-time opportunities are likely to involve Multi Level Marketing (MLM), where, as well as selling the product, you can recruit other reps. For many companies, more money can be made by recruiting than by just selling the products. Have a think about whether this appeals to you.

Research your opportunities

Contact your local rep, if you know them, and ask whether there are any opportunities in your area. A rep will be keen to recruit you if they get a bonus for this. Parenting website Netmums is a good source of info on rep opportunities, and you can find out about the experiences of people who are reps already. Look through the list of direct selling companies in this chapter, visit websites or give the company a call.

Your area

When discussing opportunities, ask what area you will cover. Some companies allocate you a street, postcode or town. Others may allow any number of reps in each locality. It pays to find how much competition there is. Think about a different company if there are several other reps nearby. The further you travel, the higher your costs, which eats into your profits.

Agent or distributor

Find out if you are becoming an agent or a distributor. As a distributor, you buy goods, and are responsible for reselling them. This has a slightly higher risk than being an agent, where you sell on behalf of the direct selling company and take a commission. Ask whether you can be a rep for another company at the same time. Selling products from more than one company can increase your income.

 Jane sells Kleeneze and Oriflame products door to door. She says, "It depends on the house whether I leave both product books or just offer one. People living in large houses may not be so interested in Kleeneze. I rarely get repeat orders from that sort of house for Kleeneze, whereas I do for Oriflame cosmetics. People on my local estate like Kleeneze but are less likely to have spare money for Oriflame, as it is more of a luxury." Jane can sell Kleeneze and Oriflame products at any time in any area, which increases her chances to earn. She also sells Usborne books. You are not allowed to sell other products alongside Usborne so she sells them at a different time and in different places. I run the three different businesses to get the most out of direct selling."

Meet your manager

Before you commit, try to meet your local manager. A good manager is there to answer your questions before you join, and support you to meet targets once you have signed up. They get an incentive to support you, such as a small percentage of your sales, so make sure you feel that the manager is offering you the help you need.

Direct Selling Association

Check whether the company is a member of the Direct Selling Association before you sign up. This means that each business complies with a code, which demands truthfulness and openness in recruitment advertisements, ensures you pay a reasonable amount to start up, and requires proper training, contracts, cancellation and buyback rights for reps, as well as prompt payment.

Start-up costs

You will be able to get started with many companies for somewhere between £25 and £50, especially if you watch out for special offers. If you have £100 or £200, you will have a wider choice of starter kits. You shouldn't have to invest more than £200 in the first week to get started.

Check the contract

Once you are happy with what you are being offered, you will be given a contract to sign. Read this carefully before you make your final decision. It should lay out your cancellation rights, how much notice you have to give if you want to stop selling, and how the company buys back unsold goods, which is required under UK law. Check if you are covered by insurance. The company should have product liability insurance, but check if you are covered by public liability insurance or whether you have to arrange this yourself. You should also be clear what percentage of sales you get. Most companies offer in the region of 15 to 40 per cent. Some offer a higher percentage for bigger orders. Ask how often commission is paid.

Ways to sell

Once you have your kit, talk to your manager about ways to sell your products. This will vary for each company. Think about who will use your products and where you might find them. According to the Direct Selling Association, about 85 per cent of sales are made in people's homes.

Door-to-door

Does the company encourage you to sell door-to-door and drop off catalogues? It can take time to build a round like this. Some people are always keen to buy, while others are never in. You need to slog round in all weather, and make repeat visits to collect catalogues, return to people who are out the first time you call, and finally to deliver the orders. Many companies require you to pay for catalogues, which gives you an extra incentive to get them back from people who are not interested.

Selling to groups

You can also sell by visiting businesses, social clubs or anywhere people gather. Do you visit toddler groups and nurseries, or could you leave a catalogue at local offices or schools? Look in your local paper and listings directories to see where other groups are held, and give them a call to see if you can attend. Visiting groups may not make great sales initially. Consider returning on a regular basis, so people know you will be there and remember to bring money to buy. You can also make the most of the opportunity when visiting a group by recruiting people to host parties.

Practical details of selling to groups

When you visit a group, make sure you have worked out the practical details. People may not have money with them at the time. Will you take orders, how will you get people to pay up, and how will you get their products to them? Make sure you keep accurate records as you go, and always have a couple of ways to contact customers who have ordered in case they are not at the group when you return.

Party planning

Selling at parties can give you the opportunity to promote

your range to a captive audience, made up of people who have come prepared to buy. Typically, around seven to eight people attend a party, and more than nine out of ten will order.

Finding hosts

When you start, write a list of friends and family who might host a party. Most companies offer a gift or incentive for the party host. Aim to recruit another couple of hosts from amongst the guests. Only six in ten parties booked end up going ahead, according to DSA research, so you need to find more potential hosts than you might think.

Get the party started

Ask the host to provide a glass of wine to start the evening off. You might do some activities to get people chatting and joining in. You will work out with a little experience just how many samples you need to get people interested. Your manager may be able to advise or help you out with your first event. An average party will generate a couple of hundred pounds worth of sales. There will, unfortunately, always be parties where no one is interested in buying.

 Caroline spent three-and-a-half years as a Pampered Chef demonstrator. She says, "I'd prepare a recipe while demonstrating the equipment. They would eat the food and place orders." Caroline didn't cover a set area, and offered parties on the nights that suited her. She says, "Because my work was commission based, it relied on me finding party hosts. My bookings were usually word of mouth so the impression I made really counted.

Building a schedule of shows each week helped me get a stable level of earnings." She continues, "It was stressful if I didn't get another booking from each show I attended, so part of my show would always be to tout for more parties. Most shows would generate one new booking and possibly two. If I took a break for a couple of weeks I'd plan some shows in advance. It can be difficult if you don't have bookings, and equally stressful when you are busy. I developed lots of skills at converting a maybe, or even a no, into a firm party booking. This gets easier with practice and training and the company also offer hosting gifts which are great to tempt people into booking. I didn't have to pay for any of these extras." Caroline is a successful rep, and comments, "There are lots of incentives to develop your business and have a busy schedule. I went to New York all expenses paid. I would never have believed I could do it, but I earned points for every pound I took, and it soon added up."

Recruitment and team building

Once you have some experience under your belt, you may want to look at ways to earn more from your business. Many companies offer the chance to increase profits by recruiting others. If you build a good team you can earn far more than you would do alone, as you get around 15 per cent of your team's takings. You need to invest time in helping them succeed. Only recruit people who you feel will make a go of it. Note that it is illegal to get people to join a scheme where they make money just from getting more people to join up.

Caroline continues, "The money is in recruiting teams of people. When I did parties, I would tempt people to join Pampered Chef with throwaway comments about how much I enjoyed the shows, how flexible the job is and what I spent my earnings on. I received a management fee which is a percentage of team members' sales. The recruits don't lose out. The money comes from the company for the extra work I do in looking after my team."

Selling 'the business opportunity'

In reality, some reps sell most in their first few weeks, and then find they have run out of friends and family to sell to. Only around a third of people joining will experience long-term success. If you struggle to sell, have a think why. Is the product something you are passionate about, and can you find other people who you think will want and be able to afford your products? If not, why not try a different company? Can you find people who you think would love your stuff, but are not managing to persuade them to buy? Talk to your manger about how to improve your selling techniques. Or, if you're not making enough money in selling products, do you need to look at recruiting other people? Think about whether you are happy to sell a 'business opportunity' alongside, or in preference to, the products you signed up to sell.

How much will I make?

With this sort of opportunity, earnings are variable. Some reps find it hard to cover the cost of their kit. Others make enough money for a few treats each month. Some invest lots of time and effort to make their sales provide several thousand pounds each year towards the family's income. In a survey the Direct Selling Association found that the average annual sales per seller, across hundreds of direct selling businesses, was £4094. Note that this is sales, not the amount you make for yourself. With commission ranging from 15 to 40 percent, average reps are making from £600 a year to just over £1600.

Work hard to earn

Direct selling companies are required by law to remind potential reps, "Do not be misled by claims that high earnings are easily achieved." Anyone who is making a good income from selling is putting many hours of effort in each month. As a rep you will most likely work on a self-employed basis. You need to register with the Inland Revenue, and are liable for paying your own National Insurance and income tax.

 Caroline stopped working as a rep when her business began to clash with her interest in ice hockey. She says, "My son started to play ice hockey as well and I started coaching his team. Together with my practice night that took up three nights each week. I combined both roles for four months, and ended up resenting being out every evening. I felt ice hockey was my real passion. It was a hard decision to make, and I miss the money. I'm going to enjoy a few months without working before looking for a job when my daughter starts school next year."

Direct sales opportunities

Read on to find out about the different opportunities available. This is not an exhaustive list, but will give you an idea of some companies with rep opportunities. To find more openings, search the internet, check out websites like Mum and Working, or contact the Direct Selling Association for a list of members.

Personal care

A great area to work in if you love cosmetics, beauty or jewellery. Make sure you try the products you will be selling, and can recommend them. Most companies in this section offer basic starter kits and more expensive versions with a bigger range. Avon has low start-up costs of just £15. Jewellery start-up kits can be a little more expensive due to the higher value products, although some offer free start-up.

Cosmetics, fragrances, skincare

- Avon **www.avon.uk.com** 01604 232425

- Body Shop at Home **www.uk.thebodyshop.com** 08459 05 06 07

- Likisma Aromatherapy **www.likisma.info** 01933 446402

- Mary Kay **www.marykay.co.uk** 0800 318 288

- Oriflame **www.oriflame.co.uk** 0845 230 2255

- Virgin Cosmetics **www.virginvieathome.com** 0845 300 80 22

Anne used to work in a bank but became disillusioned by the struggle to combine her job with her three children. She handed in her notice, and started delivering Betterware catalogues. She says, "It went well to start with, but sales tailed off and I felt I was working hard for little reward." Anne switched to Avon, and says, "I haven't looked back. I have allocated streets, so I know no one else is selling where I deliver brochures. It is great fun and you get to meet lots of people. The start-up costs were taken off my first two orders so I didn't have to pay up front. You pay a small fee for the brochures, but you can choose how many to buy, whether to sell door-to-door, to friends or offer parties. I have just started to do Sales Leadership. I get other people to join and get a small percentage of their sales. I now earn enough to pay for things for myself like haircuts, and I even fund holidays too."

Vicky Shaw, a former midwife, sells for the Body Shop at Home. Most of her sales are through parties. "I occasionally work afternoons if I am recruiting or attending an event, but I arrange this to suit my family commitments and my husband's job." she explains. Vicki looked into working as a rep when her employers were unable to offer her shifts that would fit with childcare. She says, "I never thought I would be any good in a sales role. I find no need for a hard sell. People are familiar with the products and brand, and I have surprised myself that I am good at this. There is a great programme of ongoing training and support too." Financially, Vicky was into profit after her first two parties. She says, "The basic commission is good, and my start-up kit is subsidised by the company. They don't set sales targets so I don't feel pressure to sell.

The main thing you need to succeed is a love of meeting new people. I also have a fantastic area manager. Before this I would have been sceptical about working in party plan but I would now say it is worth trying."

Hana sells Dead Sea beauty products. She enjoys the freedom she gets working for herself, and says, "I have sold many things in my time. These products worked for me, and I decided selling them would be a good way to make some money. I sell at any time, even the day after the birth of my last son." Having just had baby number four, Hana says, "I'm going to be a full-time mum again. With four children under six, I don't have time to make the business really work."

Jewellery

- Angelo Collezione **www.angelogems.co.uk** 0870 446 0910

- Chez Bec **www.chezbec.com** 0845 6520892

- Jo Magdalena **www.jomagdalena.com** 0845 225 0900

- Miglio Jewellery **www.miglio.co.uk** 0845 430 9045

- Virgin Jewellery **www.virginvieathome.com** 0845 300 80 22

House and home

There are lots of opportunities to sell products for the house and home. Some of the best known companies operate in this arena, such as Tupperware. Most companies will let you join by phone, via their website, at a recruitment meeting or through a local rep. Meeting your local manager can help you work out if you like the company and are likely to get on with the person who will be supporting you.

There are also growing opportunities in selling security products, telecoms and particularly energy sales (including gas and electricity). The supply of utilities was deregulated in 1997, making this a fast growing area, but there have also been a lot of complaints about door-to-door mis-selling.

- Amway (vitamins, cosmetics and household products) **www.amway.co.uk** 01908 629400

- Betterware (products for home and garden) **www.betterware.co.uk** 0845 125 5000

- Chocolate for chocoholics **www.chocolate-for-chocoholics.co.uk** 0118 932 1043

- Demarle (cookery workshops) **www.demarle.com** 020.7304.7092

- Enjo (chemical-free cleaning products) **www.enjo.net** 0870 900 6600

- Euphony (telecoms) **www.euphony.co.uk** 01256 857 004

- Forever Living Products **www.foreverliving.com** 01926 626 630

- Girlie Gardening (garden tools) **www.girliegardening.co.uk** 01756 79 78 77

- Herbalife (aloe vera products) **www.herbalife.co.uk** 0845 056 0606

- Kleeneze (home and health and beauty products)
  www.kleeneze.net 08703 33 66 88

- Neways (nutritional supplements and personal care)
  www.neways.co.uk 0845 601 4845

- Pampered Chef (kitchenware) **www.pamperedchef.com**
  01344 293 900

- Tomboy Tools **www.tomboytools.co.uk** 02920 814196

- Tupperware (kitchenware) **www.tupperware.co.uk** 01483
  487842

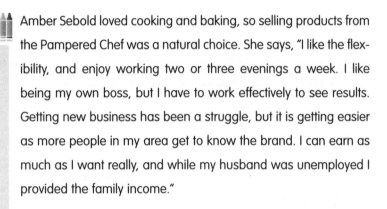

Amber Sebold loved cooking and baking, so selling products from the Pampered Chef was a natural choice. She says, "I like the flexibility, and enjoy working two or three evenings a week. I like being my own boss, but I have to work effectively to see results. Getting new business has been a struggle, but it is getting easier as more people in my area get to know the brand. I can earn as much as I want really, and while my husband was unemployed I provided the family income."

Sue Bedford works flexible hours selling eco-friendly Neways products. She says, "I was working as a hospital nurse, and wanted extra income. Now I offer health screening during school hours, and continue to boost our income with my sales of Neways products, directly and through my website, **www.healthy choices.co.uk**." Like most businesses, Sue sometimes finds sales slow. She says, "When I'm not getting regular sales from my website I place an ad in a local magazine or mention what I do on an online forum." She also focuses on customer care, saying, "A few days after someone has received an order I call to check that they are happy with their products."

Baby and child

If you've started a family you know how much equipment new babies need. There are lots of opportunities to sell baby gear, books and toys. This appeals to parents as it complements home life and they can sell products they have experienced for themselves. Choose a product you have a passion for. There is little point thinking you will do well selling cloth nappies if you have used disposables for your children. As with other areas, you will probably have to pay up to £200 for a starter kit and samples. There is one downside to working in this area. Babies grow quickly and you may have to find new customers more often than if you were selling personal care or household products.

Cloth nappies

- Babykind **www.babykind.co.uk** 0845 094 2275

- Cumfybumfy **www.cumfybumfy.co.uk** 01908 660096

- Lollipop **www.teamlollipop.co.uk** 01736 799512

- Nappy Nation **www.nappy-nation.co.uk** 0208 249 1941

- Natural Baby **www.thenaturalbabyresource.com**
  04830 84 80 50

- The Nappy Lady **www.thenappylady.co.uk** 0845 652 6532

Morag Gaherty set up The Nappy Lady after problems finding the right cloth nappy for her son. She started her adviser scheme when a friend moved from London to Wales and wanted to continue to promote cloth nappies. She shares her thoughts on what she is looking for in a nappy adviser: "Unlike many rep opportunities, we have an anti-selling approach. If you have a passion to help, you will sell nappies by default. We don't look for cloth nappy campaigners or people who are resolutely anti-disposables, but want people who can help others use the right nappy system for their circumstances." She continues, "The hours you work are up to you. Of our 50 or so advisers, some do a couple of hours a month, others work for ten or more hours a week. We look for people who are able to do local demonstrations on either a group or one-to-one basis, and can network with health professionals. You need good written English and the ability to make telephone calls. It is vitally important that you have used cloth nappies for six months or more, so you have a good basis for advising others. If you have experience of telling others about cloth nappies already, so much the better." Morag's advisers do not handle money or stock, which is administered centrally.

Ellen Madden is an agent for Lollipop cloth nappies. She combines this with working two days a week as a PA. She says, "I didn't have the funds or desire to go it alone, so being an agent for Team Lollipop is great. I have personal experience of using cloth nappies. I sell through **www.nappytastic.co.uk** and offer face-to-face advice in the evenings or weekends when my husband can care for my daughter." Ellen has found that while she took her daughter along to nappy demonstrations when she was younger, this has become more difficult. Ellen says, "She has been know to fight with clients' children and even unzipped a bean bag, sending beans everywhere." Ellen needs a car to take her kit out to customers, and says, "We only have one car, which my husband uses for work, which restricts my availability." Ellen adds, "I have only been running six months, and need to sell more nappies before I can see a profit, but I'm happy to muddle along with the business for now."

- Buggyfit (fitness for new mums) **www.Buggyfit.co.uk**
  01844 202 081

- BuyBaby (baby showers and parties) **www.buybaby.co.uk**
  0207 306 7342

- Tatty Bumpkin (yoga and activity classes)
  www.tattybumpkin.com 01732 812212

- Truly Madly Baby (baby products)
  www.trulymadlybaby.co.uk 0870 444 7207

Hannah has four children aged between one and eight, and combines looking after them with working for Truly Madly Baby. She used to work for the Body Shop at Home, and was used to selling through party plan. She swapped to Truly Madly Baby as, she says, "I have used some of the products on my own children and really knew about what I was selling." Hannah continues, "I like this because I can fit it in around my family life and even take the children along with me. You don't need any special skills, just a friendly, outgoing nature. I haven't encountered any problems, and fit in most of my work from home whilst my youngest is asleep. I'd advise anyone thinking of doing this to just be relaxed and try to keep things informal. People don't like pushy sales, but do like it when they can clearly see how passionate you are about your products." Hannah aims to recruit more consultants and ultimately become an area manager.

Children's clothes

- Captain Tortue **www.captaintortue.fr** 01903 744444

- GLOW-Inc **www.glow-inc.com** No telephone number

- Knitti **www.knitti.co.uk** 01423 551435

- Stardust Kids **www.stardustkids.co.uk** 0207 737 0199

Books, toys, games

- Barefoot Books **www.barefoot-books.com** 01225 322 400

- Child's Play books **www.childs-play.com** 01793 616286

- Fuzzy Duck **www.fuzzy-duck.co.uk** 01462 686863

- iChild **www.ichild.co.uk** 08700 705 291

- Mini IQ **www.mini-iq.co.uk** 0845 650 2044

- Tish Tash Toys **www.tishtashtoys.com** 0870 055 2072

- Usborne Books **www.usbornebooksonline.co.uk** 01484 864945 / 07968

Allison is an Usborne Books organiser. She says, "I chose to sell books as I know how much pleasure my children get from reading. I have a background working with children too. I would advise anyone to pick a product they have confidence in, as otherwise you won't be able to sell it. I mainly sell through parties, but also go to schools, nurseries, toddler groups and youth groups. I enjoy earning my own money without missing out on family life." Allison's tips if you want to do direct selling," You need good communication skills and the confidence to approach new people to hold fairs. I found it difficult to begin with but it has got easier over time." Allison also advises, "You may find some schools and nurseries already use a rep from a different company. Some of the ones I have approached will change and order from me. It is usually up to the head."

Victoria found selling Usborne books frustrating. She says, "I had contacts at various schools, but wasn't allowed to sell to them as they were assigned to other sellers. I made a bit of money from selling to Sure Starts, but found selling individual books hopeless. Nobody wanted a party. Mums in my area preferred Virgin Vie or Body Shop. I went to a few toddler groups and got the stock mauled. At one they were serving buttered toast and I was having kittens because kids were dripping it all over the place. I think I sold two books that day. I even found that the catalogues were too expensive to buy to pass on."

Other opportunities

There is a range of companies which might appeal to you. Do you fancy having saucy parties selling sexy accessories or running a murder party perhaps? Or have you got a crafty streak, and would like to sell cards or gifts? Alternatively you might fancy organising events or selling travel services.

- Ann Summers – party organiser **www.annsummers.co.uk** 0845 456 6948

- Stringfellows **www.stringfellows.net** 0845 257 0800

- Creative Memories **www.creativememories.co.uk** 01635 294700

- My Little Artist **www.mylittleartist.co.uk** 020 7193 0334

- Partylite Candles **www.partylite.co.uk** 01923 848730.

- Phoenix cards **www.phoenix-trading.co.uk**

- Blue Murder Events **www.bluemurderevents.co.uk** 07946 424 111

- Funky Mamas (events) **www.funkymamas.co.uk** 0800 169 9583

- Small Steps (magazine sales/design) **www.smallstepsmagazine.co.uk** 01386 860504 (There are more franchise magazine opportunities in the next chapter)

- Travel Counsellors **www.travelcounsellors.co.uk** 0800 195 7193

Chapter 6

Franchises

If you are looking for a business, you may have considered a franchise. You will need in the region of several thousand pounds to buy one, and you then benefit from support, national advertising, and a business model that has worked for other people. Read this chapter to find out more about the pros and cons of a franchise business.

A franchise is an opportunity for you to buy into a successful business. Someone else has come up with the idea, tested it out and hopefully made a foolproof plan you can use. If you pay for a franchise, you develop your business with the advantage of the franchisor's experience. You decide how to run it, within the limits of the franchise agreement.

The word 'franchise' describes more than one sort of arrangement. The most relevant arrangement for this book is Business Format Franchising where you pay for permission to use the trademark and logo of a business to sell a product or service. The package may also include training, product development, advertising and other promotional activities, and management systems for the business. You can run a franchise as a sole trader, in partnership, or as a limited company. (see Chapter 1)

Fees for franchising

As a franchisee you are required to pay certain fees. These can include an initial payment, monthly fees for support, a percentage of takings and renewal fees. The British Franchise Association estimates the start-up fee to be in the region of £40,000, but there are opportunities available for less than £10,000. Monthly fees vary. Some franchises require you pay up to 20 percent of your sales each month, with an average of seven or eight percent. Kumon study centre franchises are atypical, with an investment of just a few hundred pounds but monthly franchise fees of 40 to 45 per cent of the fees you receive.

How franchisors help

A wise franchisor wants to see your business succeed, as you are a source of revenue for them. When you sign up for a franchise, you will get help with setting up and running the business. They may help you find a site for your business. The franchisor may help with interior layout and design too, or could specify exactly how your premises should appear and where you should get your shop fittings from. You may get help with recruitment, marketing and advertising. Weigh up the advice and support you are getting against the fees you are paying.

What you need to succeed

If you want to open a franchise you need the initial investment to pay for the franchise and get it ready for business.

Think about costs over and above the franchise fee, such as rent and insurance. You also need to be committed to the franchise product or service. It will take many hours of hard work to get your business off the ground. You will almost certainly find you spend less time with the family than you would like at this stage.

Finding a suitable franchise

The British Franchise Association says that you can get good returns from a franchise "providing you choose a good franchise in the first place". So, how do you choose? As with any business opportunity, start by working out what you want and need. What are your skills? What sort of business could you be passionate about? What hours will work best for you? If the franchise needs to be open nine to five and weekends can you fit this in with the school run? Do you want to run the business by yourself, with a partner, or do you want to employ staff? Do you want a franchise you can run from home, or would you like to keep the business and home separate? Will you need transport for the business? And how long do you see yourself running this sort of business for? You may be signing up to a commitment for five or 10 years.

 Sarah Skelton has experienced two different franchises. The former dispensing optician worked with her first husband in their Specsavers franchise. She says, "Optics for me was only a job, never a passion. After eight years we sold the franchise and travelled around the world for three months." Sarah then had her third child, and found she needed to lose a few stone. She says, "I had seen Rosemary Conley's Hip and Thigh diet in the shops and managed to lose some weight at home, then attended a class. I was nearly at my goal weight when my instructor suggested I train to teach classes. I loved the idea, and joined the YMCA Exercise to Music intensive course, which involved seven days training, seven days at home with loads of homework then seven days back in London. I was pleased to pass first time." The family then moved house and Sarah started to think about setting up her own franchise. She says, "I knew the benefits of franchising from Specsavers. Rosemary Conley and what she stood for really appealed. I love bouncing around to music and I liked the idea of my own business. I attended a presentation in January, got accepted and was trading by that September. Setting up a business is tough under any circumstances but even tougher when you don't know the area. Working evenings was hard to start with but at least I was always there to pick the children up from school." Sarah found various problems in her first year. "I had to spend time getting known in the area and doing lots of marketing. I had difficulties finding the venues. Few people came through the door to start, yet I was paying out all the time. It took two years for me to build up a profitable business. I've now been going for nine years." Sarah has found that her franchise suits family life. She says, "My husband, Andrew, helps in the evenings when I run classes. I have found that taking out a franchise with a well-known brand name means people are already aware. I think the formula of diet and exercise is excellent and I have had great support to help build my success. My children are proud of their fit mum."

Ask around

You may have decided to find out about a franchise because you know someone who is having success already. If not, ask other people who have bought the franchise for their experiences. Ask the franchisor for statistics on take-up and how long people run franchises for. How many people have given up within the first year or three years? Why have they stopped, and did they manage to sell the franchise on? Have people bought a second franchise, and what was their motivation for this? Look at the way the business works. Can you find other businesses that have been successful with a similar format?

Strong branding?

Part of your money is paying for the brand which the franchisor has grown and developed. It is hard to measure the financial worth of a brand, so ask yourself whether you have heard of the brand. Have you seen national advertising for it? If you ask friends for a name of a few companies in the relevant sector, does that brand come up? What do people think of the company? You don't have to only consider well-known brands, but a business with a good reputation will certainly help you get your franchise off the ground.

 Helena considered running a franchise but had a few queries about how it would all add up. She says, "I looked into a magazine franchise but just didn't think it was worth it. The usual reason for a franchise is that the company you buy into is a trusted brand and advertises nationally, but with the franchise I looked at each magazine has its own name. There's no advertising of the brand. I just thought that it wasn't worth paying a whopping initial amount out and then paying each month. I also looked into a baby class franchise and I got some info about the costs. From the start-up costs, licence etc, I tried to work out the figures. I just couldn't see how you made the money, it just didn't add up, especially as I would have needed to pay interest on a loan too."

Money money money

Find out how the price of the franchise has changed over time. If the franchisor has been able to raise their prices then the franchise is becoming more valuable: conversely, a drop in prices could indicate that the business is not taking off. It pays to go through the finances in detail. Look at how much it would cost you to set up a similar business without the support of the franchisor. Could you pay for other professional support with the money you would invest in the franchise? Does the franchisor offer great prices for your stock, due to their large purchasing power?

Raising finance

What funds do you have, what can you afford to invest? Most big banks are used to potential franchisees approaching them for finance. Banks will want to see a business plan with details of your projected finances. The franchise company may have links with banks that have already lent to other franchisees. Look for a bank that has a franchise department as they will have more specialist expertise to help you.

Getting a loan

According to the British Franchise Association, banks may look on a request for a loan to start a franchise slightly more favourably than if you were starting a business alone, possibly offering more money or a lower interest rate. You will need to supply in the region of 40 percent of the start-up capital required, and the bank will loan you the rest. You will also need to have money set aside for your working capital to cover costs until money starts coming in from customers. Remember to include the monthly costs of the loan, as well as rent, utilities, insurance and franchise fees.

 Cathie Flynn researched a number of music groups before taking out a Musical Minis franchise. Her background in community art and drama made her relish the thought of running classes instead of returning to her job in finance. She says, "My husband and I were building our own house, so I increased our borrowings by a few thousand to fund the franchise fee. The equipment and training I needed to run the business were all included. I handed my notice in at work, and spent the summer looking for venues and sorting out promotion." Cathie now runs classes to fit in with her twin daughters, expanding as they moved from nursery to school. She says, "It turns out that my background was ideal for this. I applied my drama training to the classes, and use my accounts and business skills every day too."

Support and control

If you are paying for support on a monthly or annual basis,

find out exactly what you are getting. What sort of training is offered? Again, talk to other franchisees about their experiences. It is good to find out what a few different companies offer so that you can make comparisons. Find out how the franchisor controls the franchisees. What sort of financial reports will they want from you? Will they inspect the quality of what you are doing? Although this may seem onerous, it can also ensure the good reputation of the company you are buying into. Ultimately, you are putting effort into building up your business so you have a valuable capital asset.

Getting out

When you sign up for a franchise, you need to plan what will happen in the future. Are you tied in for a certain period? Many franchises are for five years. The length of the contract can reflect how long it will take you to recoup your investment and start running a profitable business, so some franchise agreements are for longer or shorter periods. What will happen at the end of the period you have signed up for? You may have the right to renew for another five years.

Your plans

Realistically, how long do you see yourself running the business? Would you want to sell it to retire, or pass it on to a family member? Find out what happens if you want to sell the business. Does the franchisor help you find a buyer if you want to sell the business, and what requirements will a new buyer have to meet?

Contracts

Check out the finances and read any contract carefully. It is essential to get legal advice from a solicitor with specialist knowledge of franchising. Contracts tend to be non-negotiable, but your adviser will help you understand what you are agreeing to. Ask your adviser to spell out hidden penalties. What happens if you fail to meet targets? How long are you committed for, and what happens at the end of that period?

Codes of ethics

Ask if the franchisor is a member of the British Franchise Association. This means the franchisor has been independently assessed against a code of ethical franchising.

Market research

Look at other franchises, and work out what makes them successful. Assess the area other franchisees are operating in, and see how it compares to where you plan to set up. Will the franchise attract business in your area? Then check whether the franchise you are interested in has availability in your locality. Are neighbouring franchises already taken and running well or will you be the first in your area?

Choose your franchise

There are nearly 800 companies offering franchises in the UK. Browse through the franchises below to see a range of options, particularly those which will appeal to parents. To find more opportunities, search the internet for sites like Which Franchise, which has extensive lists of franchise by sector and also lists home-based franchises. You can also contact the British Franchise Association and the Franchise Alliance, attend a seminar, or read one of several magazines available on the subject.

Children's physical activity

- Gymboree **www.gymboreeplayuk.com** 07967 755 008

- Little Kickers **www.littlekickers.co.uk** 01235 859 255

- Socatots **www.socatots.com** 01132 442005

- The Little Gym **www.thelittlegym-eu.com** 0208 958 7373

- Tumbletots **www.tumbletots.com** 0121 585 7003

Paul Brooker runs a Little Kickers franchise in Guildford, offering football classes for children from 18 months to five years. He says, "The beauty of what I do now is that I work when I want to and I have time to spend with my wife and son. I currently work 9am to 3pm Monday to Thursday doing admin and coach classes on Friday, Saturday and Sunday morning." Paul previously worked as a sales manager but his work-life balance was out of kilter. He says, "My wife works full-time and when our son was born we had no option but to put him into a nursery five days a week. We could not afford to lose an income. As I got promoted I often left on a Monday morning and did not return until Friday night. Lisa ended up bringing work home and completing it after bedtime. We talked continually about how to change the situation but it always came down to money. Then one day my wife said 'It's not about money, it's about us and the way we live.' We decided that one of us would change career." Paul's son already attended Little Kickers, and Paul saw they wanted more franchisees. He says, "I am football mad so it seemed too good to be true to be able to combine something you love with a job. All the figures, support and projections stacked up and so we took the plunge. Quitting my job and stepping into the unknown was the hardest thing in the world. I was giving up a fantastic salary, bonuses and a flash company car. In hindsight it was the best thing I have ever done." The advantages for Paul of this new business are many. He comments, "Instead of seeing my son for seven hours a week I now see him for seven hours a day. Lisa can concentrate on her career knowing that I am around to look after him. We have taken on an allotment which is great for him. He has swimming lessons. We go to the park and play football. Instead of fast food and takeaways I have time to cook for us all."

Other children's classes

- Jo Jingles **www.jojingles.co.uk** 01494 778989

- Kumon **www.kumon.co.uk** 0800 854 714

- Monkey Music **www.monkeymusic.co.uk** 01582 766464

- Musical minis **www.musicalminis.co.uk** 020 8868 0001

- Perform **www.perform.org.uk** 0845 400 4000

- Sing and Sign **www.singandsign.co.uk** 01273 550587

- Stagecoach **www.stagecoach.co.uk** 01932 254 333

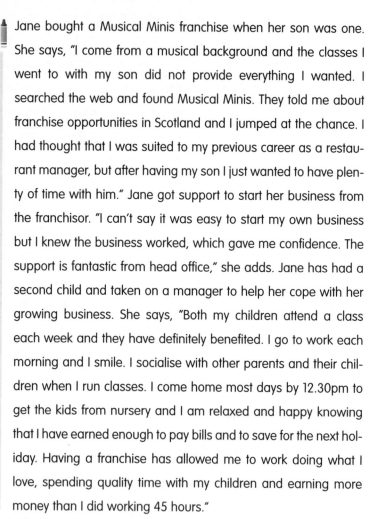

Jane bought a Musical Minis franchise when her son was one. She says, "I come from a musical background and the classes I went to with my son did not provide everything I wanted. I searched the web and found Musical Minis. They told me about franchise opportunities in Scotland and I jumped at the chance. I had thought that I was suited to my previous career as a restaurant manager, but after having my son I just wanted to have plenty of time with him." Jane got support to start her business from the franchisor. "I can't say it was easy to start my own business but I knew the business worked, which gave me confidence. The support is fantastic from head office," she adds. Jane has had a second child and taken on a manager to help her cope with her growing business. She says, "Both my children attend a class each week and they have definitely benefited. I go to work each morning and I smile. I socialise with other parents and their children when I run classes. I come home most days by 12.30pm to get the kids from nursery and I am relaxed and happy knowing that I have earned enough to pay bills and to save for the next holiday. Having a franchise has allowed me to work doing what I love, spending quality time with my children and earning more money than I did working 45 hours."

Other children's franchises

- Baby Prints **www.babyprints.co.uk** 01279 817169

- Childalert **www.childalert.co.uk** 0118 934 5893

- First Impressions **www.firstimpressions.org.uk** 020 8346 8666

- Kids Klub Videos **www.kids-klub.co.uk** 01747 853999

- Little Angels Portraits **www.littleangelsportraits.co.uk** 01242 216816

- Little Impressions **www.little-impressions.com** 0800 019 3950

Local websites and magazines

- About My Area **www.aboutmyarea.co.uk** 0870 062 2212

- The Best Of **www.thebestof.co.uk** 0121 765 5556

- ABC **www.abcmag.co.uk** 01273 542257

- My Mag **www.my-mag-uk.com** 0121 765 5555

- Families Magazines **www.familiesonline.co.uk** 020 8696 9680

- Community Times **www.mycommunitytimes.co.uk** 0800 243 462

- Family Grapevine **www.thegrapevine.co.uk** 01749 870471

- Primary Times **www.primarytimes.net** 01491 845800

- Raring 2 Go **www.raring2go.co.uk** 0121 765 5550

- Parents News **www.parents-news.co.uk** 020 8337 6337

Robina Cowan has run Families South East, a local parenting magazine, for more than ten years. She says, "My husband still has the family's 'proper' job, but I am financially self-sufficient and contribute to bills. I pay for the children's out-of-school classes, birthday presents and holiday money too." Robina took out the franchise as she wanted to be her children's main carer. She says,

"Initially I did freelance marketing and copywriting, but found I had to attend meetings at times when it was tricky to arrange child-care. When the opportunity came up to start Families South East it seemed ideal. I could use all the skills I had learnt working in PR and marketing for multinational companies." Robina enjoys being available for the children. "I arrange my work so I'm free to help on school trips, and I am there when the children return from school. I couldn't imagine going into an office, working to some-one else's schedule," she explains. On the downside, she finds "working from home can be a bit lonely. I get out every week for sports classes and belong to a networking group." Robina advis-es anyone thinking about taking up a franchise to be realistic about their strengths and weaknesses. "Get help in the areas you are not so strong, especially in the first months." Robina also sug-gests, "Draw up a list of pros and cons of setting up on your own. Give yourself plenty of time for groundwork before launching. Write a business plan, research where customers are, design and print letterheads, set up a website, and open a business bank account. A good accountant who specialises in your sort of busi-ness is invaluable. They will make your business as profitable as possible and advise you on matters such as VAT." Robina still loves the fact that she can fulfil her childhood plan to write. "Ten years on, it is still an interesting way to earn a living. As the magazine has grown I have invested in more pages, more copies, full colour. There's scope to continue with this. The balance of time for the business and 'me time' is an important factor in deciding how big I want it to be," she concludes.

Home and lifestyle

- Global Travel Group **www.globaltravelgroup.com**
  0870 429 8100

- Kings Maid **www.kingsmaid.co.uk** 0161 449 5843

- Maid2clean **www.maid2clean.co.uk** 01606 836080

- Merry Maids **www.merrymaids.co.uk** 0116 275 9000

- Molly Maid **www.mollymaid.co.uk** 0800 500950

- My home **www.myhomeplc.com** 08450 693369

- Revitalise **www.revitalise-franchise.co.uk** 01273 738230

- Rosemary Conley **www.rosemary-conley.co.uk**
  01509 622000

- Topmatch UK Dating **www.topmatch-uk.com**
  08707 203 270

- Travel Counsellors **www.TravelCounsellors.co.uk**
  0800 195 7193

More areas in which you can find franchises

Car cleaning and repair	Gardening
Dating	Greeting card distribution
Delivery and van based businesses	Allergy testing
Estate agent and property services	Health and beauty
Takeaways and restaurants	Nutrition
Finance	Pets and animal care
Will writing	Recruitment

Marc was a store manager, but wanted to work for himself. He looked at various franchises, and decided a van-based business would work for him. He says, "I was worried about the expense of new premises, but saw that if I went for an Agency Express franchise, providing and erecting 'For Sale' boards for estate agents, I could run the business from home." Marc says, "An experienced member of Agency Express spent three days with me visiting local estate agents to introduce my service." Marc has now been running the business for more than five years. He says, "It took a while to build up, but estate agents' recommendations meant the business started growing. Being part of a national network helped, especially the professional image of the logoed vans." He goes on to say, "I enjoy the freedom of being my own boss and find I have more time to spend with the family. The business has grown steadily. I now have two part-time staff and two vans on the road, each van handling an average of 30 to 40 jobs a day. There's still room for growth and I aim to add a third van next year."

Setting up a franchise

You may be reading this chapter not because you want to buy a franchise but because you see yourself as a franchisor, licensing out your business to other people. If you want to do this you will need legal and financial advice. There are specialist companies who help set up franchise operations. Read about one mum who has run a business offering franchises for more than ten years, and another two parents who are just starting out.

Karen Sherr started Musical Minis 18 years ago, and has been offering franchises since 1997. She says, "I was a Play Specialist at Great Ormond Street Hospital. I had intended to return after having Matthew but I didn't like the idea of leaving him. I took Matthew to an exercise group where the song at the beginning and the end of each session was his favourite part. I tried to find him a fun local music group but with no luck. I started to miss being surrounded by a ward full of children. This mixed in with my inability to find a suitable music group, and knowing some of my friends were also interested in a music group, led to the launch of Musical Minis." Karen devised a programme for the classes, bought the equipment, hired a hall, and took out insurance. Karen says, "We had one session a week, and a leader at the exercise group came on board as my partner. When she took the class, Matthew and I could take part." The classes became popular, and Karen took on more staff. She worked through two more pregnancies, and took seven years to create her first franchise. She says, "We wanted to set up everything legally before we offered the franchise for sale. We had to register our trademark. We became embroiled in a dispute which we won, but the process took a long time. Our music needed to be cleared. We hired a recording studio with singers, so we own the recordings. We then had to create the lesson tapes, apply for a licence, duplicate the tapes and pay royalties." There were also other arrangements to be set in place. "We liaised with lawyers to create a franchise agreement, wrote clear operating and training manuals. We run training sessions to help franchisees with any problem using our first-hand experience." Financially, starting the franchise business has been a big commitment for Karen and husband Rob. It cost in the region of £50,000 to set up. Karen says, "At first we worried we had taken on too much. Now we can take money out of the business and not reinvest everything. We could have grown much faster and taken on more franchisees but we wanted the business growth to fit in with the family. We also wanted to be able to support each franchisee fully." Musical Minis currently has nearly 20 franchisees in the UK, running classes from 98 different venues each week, as well as 17 Sure Starts licensed to offer the classes. It costs between £5,000 and £10,000 for a five-year licence to run a Musical Minis franchise. Franchisees earn on average £15,000 a year.

Alison and Jaci run an independent community magazine business. They set up with two magazines, then took on a franchisee. Alison says, "We did a lot of research online and bought an off-the-shelf franchise agreement, which we modified to our requirements. Jaci is a trained accountant which helped. Our franchisee started her magazine about a year ago when she was working and the business has been successful enough for her to give up her job. Our approach as franchisors is different to many. Our main priority is to have a good, part-time job and time for our families. If we had taken on dozens of franchisees we would not have been able to develop our magazines 'Bradley Stoke Matters', and 'Little Stoke Gifford Matters' and our community website, **www.bradleystokematters.co.uk**. We have been able to give practical hands-on advice, support and guidance to our franchisee, which has contributed to the success of her magazine. Our pricing structure for franchisees is set up with only a token up-front payment, followed by a percentage of monthly revenue. We looked for a franchisee who was community-minded, with drive and all-round business sense. From an ethical point of view we don't end up taking money from someone unsuitable for the role and wasting their money and our time. The onus is on us to dedicate time and effort in helping our franchisees build their business, which in turn benefits us through a higher monthly revenue, greater job satisfaction and a reputation for high quality, successful magazines. We plan to take on more franchisees, one at a time. Once we've assessed the success of our website, we will trial a site with our current franchisee and then add this as an option for future franchisees."

Chapter 7

Web-based business

The internet makes it possible to reach far more customers than you would in your local area. From single auctions on eBay to large online stores shifting thousands of items each day, more and more people are selling via the web.

This way of selling has enormous advantages for mums and dads. You can run an online business from home. It is possible to work mostly by email, so no one will hear the children in the background, and you can fit your work in at the time that suits you. This chapter outlines how to sell online through other people's websites, and how to set up your own site. Read on to find how other parents have set about it too.

Bonita Birkett runs an online store specialising in items for twins, called Twinsthings. She explains how she got started: "After having my twins I spent ages trawling the shops and web to find things to make life a bit easier with two babies and found that most things for twins were only available in the US. I was also frequently asked where to get things by other parents of twins, so came up with the idea for the business. I had a well-paid career, but was no longer happy in it after having my babies and felt I was missing out on too much by working such long hours, so took the plunge to make the change and started running the business from home."

Gill Hunt runs Skillfair, an online service which helps companies find high quality, skilled specialists, and finds new clients for consultants. She says, "I set up the website because I saw a gap in the market and it offered a new challenge." She enjoys the flexibility of working from home and reckons she saves several hours a week by not having to commute. On the downside, Gill says, "Clients call on a Friday night when everyone wants to relax for the weekend. I've got a second phone line to get round the problem of my children answering the phone, and we've ended up building an extension so I have space to work. We're just about to invest in a virtual phone network that will let all of the team answer the phone. We have people with children from two to 16, and all have different times of day that are 'good' so between us we cover most of the day."

eBay and other internet selling

Everyone has heard of eBay, most people have bought something through the online auction site, but have you sold anything yet? It is simple to sell items, and many people just sell unwanted possessions. There are other online auction sites which work in similar ways to eBay with small variations, but eBay is by far the most popular and successful. This section concentrates on getting started selling through eBay.

Other online auction and sales sites:

- QXL UK **www.qxl.co.uk**

- eBid UK and overseas sites **www.eBid.co.uk**

- Amazon Marketplace UK and overseas sites
  www.amazon.co.uk

- CQOut UK and overseas sites **www.cqout.com**

- Visit **www.auctionlotwatch.co.uk** for a longer list of auction
  sites. They have a separate category for new sites and those
  with fewer than 500 bids, so you can find established sites.

Auctioning on eBay

First of all, what are you going to sell? You may want to trawl
car boots and charity shops for items you think are cheap and
would sell for more. This is a gamble, but you may develop a
feel for what sells. It is easier if you have some sort of specialist knowledge or can develop a niche area.

Get crafty

Alternatively, you may be creative and make something which
you want to sell online. Make sure you cost your time and
materials carefully. A common pitfall is to undervalue handmade items. Or, you may want to buy new items wholesale
and sell them on at a marked up price. You can sell items for a
fixed or 'buy it now' price on eBay as well as by auction.

Start to sell

If you want to try out selling, go to **www.ebay.co.uk**. Click on

'Sell'. Fill in your name and contact details to set up an account if you are not already registered. Then, write a few key words for your auction title. Think of what people might search on if looking for your item. Select the categories you want it to appear in. For example, if you are selling toy trains you may want to feature in children's toys, in 'pre-school' toys, and also if your trains are from a popular brand, under the appropriate brand category.

Then tick a box to indicate whether the product is new or used. Write a careful description of the item. This is the place to point out what is great about your item, and highlight any faults if the item is second-hand. You have the option of selling multiple items too.

Pricing your item

Decide how you want people to buy the item. You can select an auction, or offer it at a fixed price, which is used more often if you have a number of new items to sell. If auctioning the item, set a start price. You have the option of offering a 'buy it now' price, which the buyer can select if there have been no other bids. The 'buy it now' price automatically ends the auction, so set it at a level at which you would be happy to sell the item.

When setting your price, research how much other similar items have sold for. There is the facility to 'search' through auctions on eBay. Include completed auctions in your search, so you can see final prices for a range of items.

You can also choose a reserve price. If, for example, you start an auction at 99p to attract lots of interest, you may not actually want to sell the item for less than £50. You therefore set the reserve price at £50. If the auction ends and the bids have not reached £50, bidders will be notified that the reserve has not been met. You can then list the item again.

Timing

Then, choose how long you would like the auction to run for. You can delay the start of the auction, for a small fee. There are key bidding times, and it can be more profitable to end your item at a time when lots of people are online and bidding. Most people are online weekend evenings, so this is a good time to start and end a one-week auction. You may want to refine this for your particular products. Someone targeting mums with new babies may find more of them online during the day.

Auction fees

EBay charges a fee for you to list each item. This starts from a few pence and increases as the starting price, or reserve price, goes up. You then also pay around five per cent of the final sale price, if the item sells. If you relist an item that has not sold, you will have to pay the listing fees again, although these are refunded if the item sells second time around. You pay more if you are listing multiples of one item. The final value fees vary to some extent for books, CDs and DVDs, and technology items. You can find out more on eBay itself.

Pictures sell

You have the option of adding pictures to your auction. Clear images will greatly help your chances of selling your item. Buyers prefer to bid on something they can see. The first image is free, then you pay a few pence for each additional image, and more for a more prominent 'gallery' listing.

Feedback

Once you start buying and selling on eBay you will get 'feedback', short comments and a positive, neutral or negative rating from the people you have dealt with. The more feedback you have, the more confident buyers feel, although obviously a system like this is not foolproof.

Payment and delivery

You need to select how people can pay you. EBay's preferred method is PayPal, which allows you to send and receive money instantly by email. You can also offer payment by cheque or postal order, but will need to allow time for people to post the cheque. More buyers fail to pay this way, simply because of the effort of remembering to write and post the cheque. You can also offer payment by credit card. There's more about payment methods later on in this chapter.

Post and packaging

When you create an auction you also need to lay out how much postage and delivery will cost the buyer. You need to allow a small amount for the cost of the packaging, on top of the basic postage. You can also set up rules so people get a discount on postage if they buy more than one item.

 Claire sold a few items she didn't want on eBay while she was expecting her son, to pay for baby equipment. She says, "Soon I was scouring boot sales and charity shops for more things to auction. I got a thrill when something I bought cheaply sold for a profit. It helped us at an expensive time." Claire found that Adam grew out of his clothes quickly so she could sell those too. And when her second child came along, Claire wondered if she could fund some unpaid maternity leave by selling on eBay. She was mainly buying and selling baby and children's products by this stage, so started investigating children's wear and baby products wholesalers. At the same time, she was offered redundancy, which was just the spur she needed. "Instead of going back to work for someone else, I launched a business selling maternity wear, baby and children's equipment and clothes online. eBay had been fun, but it was time to step up a gear. I'd found that as eBay got busier the quality of goods was dropping too." Claire's baby business was her sole source of income for a number of years. She has now returned to employment. "Selling online was a good way to earn a living while the children were little, but it was hard work, with no security."

Simple selling

The process to sell on eBay seems quite complex the first time you do it, but you will get faster with practice. There are tools to help you list lots of items, such as Turbo Lister. Don't underestimate the length of time it will take to photograph and upload your images, handle enquiries and payment, pack the items and take them to the post office.

eBay shops

One way to have your own online store is to set up an eBay shop. You get a customisable "shop front" page on eBay, and can add your own logo. Shops cost from a few pounds up to several hundred pounds a month. The advantage is that your products are included when people search eBay. However, setting up your own website gives you greater flexibility.

Your own online shop

Nowadays it is relatively straightforward to get your own website, with a shopping cart to allow people to purchase from you. While many people just stick with selling on eBay, your own site can give you far more options, and people may perceive your operation as more professional. This section tells you how to go about setting up your own website, and how some other parents have done it.

 Natasha Rushbrook runs an online retail outlet that sells baby gift, toy and nursery products. She says, "I started Stork Gifts as I felt that I was just a wife and mum. People had forgotten I had skills." Natasha enjoys the flexibility of running her own business online, but admits that there are tensions with family life. "As the business grows it needs more attention. I've felt that I am neither a proper stay-at-home mum nor a full-time working mum. I've had to make some tough decisions about whether to move forward with the business or to stop altogether." She says, "After a long hard think I have decided that I can't stay where I am, with just an online business. This year I'm planning to open a shop, finish off a catalogue and take sales forward in new and different directions. To do this I've had to give up being a full-time mum to my kids although I am around more than if I was working out of the home."

Names and web addresses

It is important to decide on a name for your business. When you have a few ideas, check with Companies House that there are no other companies with the same name operating in the same line of business. Visit Nominet online to ensure that the name you are after is available as a domain name. It is a bad idea to start a business without having registered the domain name. You may find someone else snaps up the name you want and you risk having to pay over the odds to get it back.

Sadie and Justin Knight run a web design company, **www.glass-raven.com**, which Sadie started after she had her daughter. Sadie says, "My path to self-employment started in 1999 when I was pregnant with my daughter Callista. I started learning how to design websites, initially to share photographs with friends and family, and then for friends' water diving business. I was then asked to do a site for the Centre for Environmental Research at Coventry University. I applied to a local web design firm for a week-long assignment they had advertised. I completed the work in a day and a half and was asked to come back on a part-time basis during my university vacations. This gave me a great insight into the world of web design and graphics, but it didn't really occur to me to work for myself until after I gave birth to Aiden a month early in October 2001. I was still working on a couple of projects for the firm so finished them off working from home, and then the realisation hit that this was something I could do around the children, who were at that time four months and almost two." Five years down the line, Sadie's husband Justin has taken redundancy and Glassraven supports the family.

Online branding

You also want to develop a 'look' for your online business. To start with, do a little research on the internet. Look at other websites and see what appeals to you. Which sites do you feel confidence in, and which would you not want to buy from? Look at business logos, and the different colours and styles used on various websites. This will help you develop the way your online store will look.

 Alison Berry had a background in the toy industry, which she put to good use in her online business, idealpresent, **www.idealpresent.co.uk**, a free online gift advice service. Alison says, "You answer some questions about the child you're buying for, then idealpresent tells you what to buy, and where to buy it." Alison's website brings her an income while giving her the time to spend with the family that she wanted. "The business provides an income stream with next to no over-heads or running costs. My objective in setting up the business was to use my skills and experiences, whilst having a career which fitted around our family life." It can be hard to make a profit from this sort of website, where the customer receives a service for free. Alison has managed this with a range of income routes. She says, "idealpresent is a member of several affiliate schemes. When gifts from certain retailers are recommended this links directly through to the retailer. If people click through and buy, idealpresent gets commission. I was keen not to have adverts all over the site. The other income stream is 'seeding'. Retailers or manufacturers pay to have their products featuring at the top of the recommendations list or on the 'what's hot' section."

Logo

A logo will help customers recognise your business. You can use it on your website and business stationery. You may want to create your own logo, sketch something out and get a designer to formalise it for you, or ask a professional designer for ideas. There are various websites which help you create logos too, including Cooltext, for text only logos, **www.cooltext.com/Logos**, and Logoyes where you pay a fee for a high resolution logo, **www.logoyes.com.**

DIY or pro

Have a think about whether you want to design the site yourself or get a professional to do it for you. Do you have the time and skills to do it yourself? There are lots of resources to help you online, and you can read below about how some business owners have learnt to create and manage their own sites. If you want to find a designer, there are lots of business directories online.

Bex Smith has designed her own websites. She says, "I use Mozilla composer, which is free for all my site stuff. I have found it easy to learn 'on the job', and have learnt a fair bit along the way about HTML too, although I still claim to be an HTML dunce. When I started doing my site I think I paid about £80 for a template which I have hashed about a few times to make the looks I want for my various sites."

Creating your own site

If you want to create your own website, it is useful to know something about HTML(hyper text markup language). This is the language websites are written in. Depending on your interests and skills you can create a site entirely in HTML, or use a WYSIWYG (what you see is what you get) editor which shows you what the page will look like, rather than the code which is behind it. This sort of programme makes it easier for novices to create their own site. Look at free editor NVU, or buy a programme like Dreamweaver. When you have made your site, don't forget to check that it looks good in browsers like Firefox and Safari, as well as Internet Explorer.

 Sue says, "I produced the websites myself using Serif Page Plus and WebPlus software. I did a short web design course for small businesses at my local college, funded by the European Social Fund, which taught me basic HTML. I enjoy creating websites so I decided to do it all myself and it is easy to maintain and update them. My main problem has been optimising them for search engines with finding the right keywords. It has helped by using reciprocal links with other websites and directories."

Miranda Stamp has done a lot of work on her own websites, and has found some helpful resources. She says, "The best book on websites I've ever bought is Creating Web Sites – The Missing Manual, by Matthew MacDonald. It's written in English not geeks-peak and has clear explanations and examples of what to write and how it will appear. It tells you the most technically correct way of doing things. For general HTML info I have also got Head First HTML with CSS and XHTML, by Elisabeth Freeman and Eric Freeman. This has a lot of good graphics and clear explanations, and exercises to do along the way. It is the sort of book you need to read without interruption." Miranda also recommends computer magazines. She says, "Magazines often include free discs with software for editing your site. A trial of something like Dreamweaver is a good way to see if you want to buy the full version. This was how I started doing my websites." Miranda has more advice, "See what short courses your local college runs. If you have no knowledge of the subject whatsoever a course will be a good way to get some basic training and an understanding of your software. You may also be able to get some training via Business Link or over the internet. You could select the programme you use on the basis of the training you can get."

More resources to help you create a website

There are a number of packages that help you set up an online shop. These packages usually include a shop front, a shopping cart system, and some also include hosting. Most can integrate with payment gateways such as PayPal, Nochex and Protx. Prices vary enormously, so check out the different features you get. Oscommerce is 'open source', which means it is free. Some systems have more flexibility, and a basic system may not serve your business if it grows. You may need to pay more for a fully customisable set-up so your online shop doesn't look similar to others with the same system.

- Mr Site **www.mrsite.co.uk**

- Store2go **www.store2go.net**

- EKMPowerShop **www.ekmpowershop.com**

- Moonfruit **www.moonfruit.co.uk**

- Romancart **www.romancart.com**

- Oscommerce **www.oscommerce.com**

- Zencart **www.zencart.co.uk**

- Actinic **www.actinic.co.uk**

Bex says, "I didn't like Oscommerce as you need the site to be in php, which is way beyond my comprehension. I settled on Romancart as I found it easy to work with. It is all copy and paste HTML stuff which suits my non-techy brain."

Nadine says, "I opted for EKMPowershop when I knew I only had five days to get a decent looking website. The features included were fantastic. It took one click to set up Protx, PayPal, and telephone ordering. It cost me £50 set-up fee, £25 per annum for the domain name and then £20 per month. It is fully hosted as well so I don't need to pay for web space either. I'd had a bit of a play with their demo site before I bought and it is idiot proof. I looked at Oscommerce but I knew I didn't have enough time to get my head around it in the timescale."

Miranda says, "I spent a few months reading all the forums, magazines etc, and Actinic was consistently recommended. It came with various templates, was relatively easy to use, and the telephone, email and forum support is excellent. Importantly it seems to work well with the search engines. Over the years I've upgraded to later versions, and it now has some excellent features. The latest version integrates with Dreamweaver so you can produce any design you like. I've also bought various time-saving additions such as integrating with Sage Line 5. This gives us stock control. You don't need to know HTML or anything complicated. It has boxes so you can add descriptive text, pictures and prices. If you do know a little HTML you can customise it easily."

Webhosting

You will need webhosting, which is some 'virtual space' for your website. You may get space included with your email account, but will probably need to switch to paid hosting if you are serious about your business. A growing website will quickly use up any free space. Free hosting also often comes with advertisements, which can make your site look less professional.

Legal requirements for selling on the net

There are certain requirements you must meet when selling over the internet. Your website must list full contact details including a name, email and geographic address. You need fair and meaningful terms and conditions too. You need to be clear about what you are offering, and how much it costs, as well as fees for delivery and taxes. Explain how the ordering process works, and what the customer should do if dissatisfied. Send a confirmation to each customer after they order. Customers have a right to cancel within seven working days for most good and services.

Privacy

You should have a policy on privacy: how you safeguard customers' contact details. You may need to comply with the Data Protection Act. Only collect information you need from your customers, and be clear that everything you are collecting has a purpose. Tell your customers what information you will keep and why. Ensure that information is kept securely, and that customers are clear about when you will share their information and who with. Find out more about this at the Information Commissioner's Office, **www.ico.gov.uk.**

Standards

Make sure you display any professional bodies you belong to and details such as VAT registration. Talk to your local Business Enterprise Agency, visit the Trading Standards website or the Office of Fair Trading website for fuller information.

 Karen Thornton Brown runs **www.weddingsabroad.com**, arranging weddings all over the world. She explains how she came up with her business concept, "Whilst planning our wedding I spent several years researching various countries. The wedding planner we used in Australia asked me to consider becoming their UK agent as they had never encountered such an organised bride." The internet helped Karen get her business off the ground. She says, "I needed support from my husband, but with some self-help books and a copy of Frontpage I managed to set up my own website. Initially I only knew how to send emails and surf the web. I learnt how to do web design, create documents, spread-sheets and do all things technical in a short space of time. I have now had the website professionally designed, but managed with my own designs for eight years, and still achieved number one placement on Google." Karen knew that she wanted a family, and decided that an internet based business would allow this. "Running my business online would allow me to work from home whilst bringing up children. In my line of work office hours are not essential, but as many clients are not from the UK flexibility is vital. When my children were babies I was able to work whilst they slept. I changed the whole format of my business to enable my overseas representatives to work directly with the clients thus allowing me more time with the family. Now, though, my five year old daughter understands that Mummy plans weddings. She accompanies me on business trips, and is looking forward to working with me when she gets older." Karen also runs a web directory of wedding suppliers worldwide, and another company offering luxury villa and apartment rentals.

More features for your website

There are lots more features you may want to have built into a website. A web statistics programme will tell you how many people have visited your site, what they have looked at, where they found your site and much more. This really helps you make your site work well and tell what online marketing works too.

Taking payments

You need to be able to take payments, and most businesses with an online presence will want people to be able to pay through the website. PayPal is one of the simplest systems to set up, and charges a small percentage for each transaction. You could also look at setting up a merchant account with your business bank and using a secure online payment gateway like WorldPay, Protx or Streamline. This is more flexible than PayPal, but you will need to pay a fee of around £20 a month. This may include a certain number of transactions, after which there are further charges per transaction. Other schemes just charge you per transaction.

 Michaela Smith from Nappies by Minki has had a new website designed for her business. Her first site told customers all about the company and the products on offer, but the shopping site was hosted elsewhere, and people had to click through to this second location to shop. The new site has a fully integrated shopping cart. Michaela says, "It's much easier to view and buy online, and the new site has quadrupled retail sales."

Blogs

A blog, or weblog, can be a useful addition to your site. It's like an online diary where you can easily type in news and upload images. Many blogs are free, with the option to pay a few pounds a month for features like more space for images.

Keep it fresh

You may want to think about what else you can offer on your site. Keep it updated and add new items to attract people back. Think about using regular offers and promotions. Ask site visitors for their contact details and send out a regular newsletter. Some businesses also have more than one website, as different set-ups will attract different people.

Liz Stuart of Power Pramming runs exercise classes for new mums. She has created a DVD which extends the exercises in Power Pramming to indoors. She offers advice on her website, and will send fact sheets to mums who don't live near a class and would like to do an informal workout by themselves or with friends. This means Power Pramming can offer something for every visitor to the website.

Miranda Stamp's main website is **www.twinkleontheweb.co.uk**, selling nappies and eco-friendly products. Miranda also created **www.chooseanappy.co.uk**. She says, "This is designed to help people who are thinking of using cloth nappies and want advice. They respond to some questions and the website suggests a few types of suitable nappy. They can then click through to my main website if they want to buy." Miranda has also created How to Nappy, a website based on her booklet of information about washable nappies. Again this is designed to be found by people searching for instructions on how to use washable nappies, by answering questions such as how to fold traditional terry squares. This site will have an online shop so that viewers wanting to make purchases can do so. Miranda is also aiming to attract further visitors to her business with **www.nappyauctions.co.uk,** a site for auctioning cloth nappies. This will feature adverts linking to p roducts sold on the main Twinkle site, and there will also be a forum **www.nappynatter.co.uk** to build a community talking about nappies and encourage repeat visits, with links back to Twinkleontheweb and the other sites.

Anne Dhir of Calin Bleu retails and wholesales baby carriers. Alongside her own website, **www.calinbleu.com**, Anne also runs **www.slingmeet.co.uk**. Anne says, "Sling Meet enables parents who are into baby wearing to meet up. New parents can get advice and try out slings at the get togethers which are organised by members through the website." Sling Meet carries advertisements for Anne's business, and she feels it helps to attract visitors to her website. Anne says, "Sling Meet allows me to build relationships with other vendors and manufacturers. Magazines are happy to feature it as it's not for profit, which allows us to promote baby wearing where paid advertisement would be expensive and not have the same impact. It's also nice to meet people and make a difference locally. I'm passionate about baby wearing. Whether it's our products or another brand, I love helping mums learn to carry their children and meet up with other mums to support each other. Sling Meet allows me to do that." Anne also always tries to have plenty going on at the Calin Bleu website. She says, "We run competitions, have colouring pages and special offers too."

Online marketing

Once you have a website, you need to get it known. When creating your site you need to think about Search Engine Optimisation (SEO). The words on your site, and the 'tags' used in your website coding are picked up by search engines. SEO means planning the wording carefully to ensure your site is picked up by people using search engines to trawl for relevant terms.

 Gill Hunt markets Skillfair using a mixture of on and off line methods. She says, "Having good content accessible to the search engines has boosted us up the results pages. We use Google Ads for targeted campaigns, and online PR where we post articles on other websites and in people's email newsletters. Offline we do a mix of direct mail, telemarketing and traditional PR plus lots of networking. One of the most effective things we do is registering people for our email updates. We then have the opportunity to send them emails every few weeks when they first find us telling them about the service and why they should join."

Alison promotes her website in a range of ways, "I take any opportunity to talk to people about the business and respond to online requests for case studies. I regularly undertake research with idealpresent users about present-buying occasions, and then make these into interesting press releases and stories. I write gift guides for key occasions such as Christmas, which are published in parenting magazines and websites. I have flyers and business cards which I hand out, or site at key events and places. I've been known to go round the car park at Legoland when we're visiting, putting them on car windscreens. The most effective piece of promotion was when the idealpresent.co.uk was featured on the BBC's Click programme last year and described as "a great website". I had sent emails to the programme asking them to feature it – then I asked some friends and relatives to email them too! After about 18 months of trying, it was featured."

Online networking

When you are promoting your website it is worth networking online. Look for forums frequented by your customers. Join up, offer helpful advice where you can, and get to know what people are looking for. Forums have varying rules about promoting your own business so check the regulations before mentioning your business. There are also small business forums. These can be an invaluable source of help and advice, especially if you are starting a business from home and feel isolated.

 Sadie Knight says, "In order to build up a decent portfolio of web designs I started networking with other mums working from home and people starting up in business. I offered design work in exchange for their skills, or at reduced fees in exchange for feedback and comments for my website portfolio." Sadie has found that client referrals play a huge part in Glassraven's success. She says, "I would say that 80 percent of my clients are people who have been referred to me by a happy customer. The remaining 20 percent come from search engines where I rank well for my main targeted key phrases, or people viewing a website I have designed and clicking on my link at the bottom to approach me about doing them a site."

Chapter 8

Growing your business

What are your plans for your business? Some people start an enterprise purely to provide a little bit of extra income, but many have big plans. In this chapter you can hear from parents who own businesses that are supporting the family. Some started off knowing that they wanted a high growth enterprise, while other businesses have developed as a result of redundancy. Read on to find out some of the challenges you come across when you aim high.

Do you know you want to grow?

You may have a great idea for a business, a unique product, or a service you think everyone needs. Your business may be up and running already. But how do you know you want your business to grow? It may happen organically, and as your children get older and you have more time, you find the business expanding. Alternatively, you may be carefully planning each year's growth over five or ten years. Read on to find how some parents started a growing business.

Stuart and Lynda Howard started Free Range Kids when their first daughter was in nappies. They couldn't find the eco-friendly alternatives they wanted in the UK, so Lynda started shipping in stuff she liked from around the world. Stuart was still in full-time work at this point. He says, "I wondered what Lynda was up to on the PC late at night. Parcels arrived from the US, and it soon became clear they weren't just for Sophie. When Lynda explained her idea of an online store selling ethical baby items like carriers and nappies I was sceptical." However, Stuart soon got involved. He says, "I was offered redundancy as part of a company restructure, and it seemed like the ideal opportunity to change the way we lived. Friends who had left already told me they never regretted it. I wanted to be around for the kids instead of being in an office all day, so Lynda and I joined forces to work on the business together." It took a little while to work out different roles. Now Lynda offers customers specialist advice, researches new product lines and development opportunities and handles online marketing and presence on forums. Stuart handles more of the administration and orders, and is also responsible for consumer and trade shows. Stuart says, "It is sometimes strange being at home all the time. I need to get out to socialise. Work sometimes follows me out. One of the people I meet to play role playing games is an experienced local businessman. He's often a source of great advice as he's been through most things in his time."

Michaela Smith started Nappies by Minki in 2002, sewing custom and embroidered cloth nappies. She was joined in the business by husband Rod in 2006 after the company he worked for closed. Michaela says, "I felt total terror when we realised Rod's job was gone. His salary covered essentials, like the mortgage, food and bills. The profit from my business went to pay for extras like holidays and nice clothes." Rod looked round for other jobs, but opportunities were limited on the Isle of Lewis. Swiftly, Michaela and Rod realised that this might be the moment for Rod to start working at Nappies by Minki. Rod says, "Michaela and I have a great relationship, but we didn't know if we could be together 24/7. What would we have to talk about each evening if we were working together all day? And could the business support the family?" To add to the pressure, Michaela and Rod had recently extended the family finances to buy a new property. The plus point of the new place was that it had outbuildings, so there was plenty of space for the business to grow. Michaela continues the tale. "The business was ready for expansion. I was working at capacity, four hours a day cutting fabric, and four hours in the office. The sewing was done by outworkers. Now, I've taken Rod on as an employee. He gets a wage, and we get working families' tax credits. Rod has taken over the cutting and deals with packing orders. He handles whatever needs doing bar the office, which is my domain." Having more time in the office has enabled Michaela to grow the business. She says, "Before, I had reached the point where I wouldn't take on more wholesalers. We couldn't handle more bulk orders. In the few months after Rod came on board we added a couple of new wholesalers to the 30 or more we have across the world. We have a faster turnaround time too." The change has been successful for Rod and Michaela. Rod says, "I love it. I've had two job offers in the last month and turned them both down." Michaela says, "Our worries were unfounded. We work together well, and still have enough money to pay the bills and have a bit left over to go for a beer when we want. I'm calmer, and it's nice not working on my own all the time."

What do you need to grow?

Developing a business that will support the family needs a lot of input. In this chapter we will examine the commitments and financial input in making a successful business, and important issues such as pricing, insurance, premises, stock, staff and promotion.

 Nadine knew from the beginning she was serious about business. She advises, "Making the move from a lifestyle business to one which is revenue focused is stressful. Think about whether you want a business which just supports your lifestyle or whether you are prepared to focus on profits and margins. And hard work isn't enough – you have to want the business to succeed from your inner core.

Loubna Alachbili and her husband run a hair and beauty salon. Loubna says, "My husband and I started our own business when our son was 14 months. I work six days per week and my husband worked every day for the first four years. Now he works six days too. I went back to work three weeks after the birth of my daughter, with her in my arms. I would be breastfeeding her and working on the computer or on a business phone call, changing nappies in between meeting or interviews. She is now four and still comes with me to work on Saturdays. I can bring my seven year old boy in on school inset days. This is how we balance work and bringing up two kids."

Jean and Sam run antenatal classes. Jean says, "It's not a hobby any longer. Now I take my two pre-schoolers to nursery on the days I work. Having said that, the two youngest are quite good at knowing that they need to be quiet if mummy is working on the phone, as they have grown up with it. My older two are far more likely to interrupt." If you're thinking of growing a business, Jean says, "you may think you can work from home without childcare. I would find it hard if my kids weren't out of the house for the majority of the time I work. On the plus side, I love seeing them when they have finished school or nursery and I have finished my day's work."

It is vitally important to get a few things in place if you are serious about business. In Chapter 4 we touched on protecting your trademarks and designs. It can be costly to contest copycats, and trademarking will make it easier. The bigger you get, the more sense it makes to register as a company, especially if you are borrowing to fund your business. If the business has difficulty paying its creditors, your personal property is not at risk.

Nadine says, "If you are planning to sell the business, even in 10 years, it should influence your business planning. Make sure you develop a strong brand, and register and protect your trademark and designs. A potential purchaser for a business will look at the value of the machinery you own, other equipment, patterns, and of course, a database of your existing customers.

Insurance

Insurance is also important. Depending on your business, you may need product liability insurance or public liability insurance. See the How To guide at the end of the book for more on this.

 It took Sam and Jean several months to source insurance for their private antenatal classes, as few companies were willing to cover their work with pregnant women. Jean says, "We have two million pounds worth of cover, but have to pay a lot for it."

Financing growth

Working out how to finance the growth of your business can be a headache. There is a number of ways to get finance. Ask your local Enterprise Agency about sources of grants. These often require match funding, where you provide an amount to equal the grant. Some people use personal savings, which they loan to the business. In the early stages banks may encourage you to take out a small personal loan or extend the mortgage on your house. This makes you personally responsible for the debt. Read on to find out about the sort of investments you can get if you have a company.

 Nappies by Minki got a couple of thousand pounds from the Highlands Enterprise Agency when starting up. Michaela says, "That is the only external investment we've needed. The local business adviser can't believe we have grown so much without a bank loan. In all honesty, I didn't even consider approaching a bank. The business has developed gradually and we have invested the profits in growth."

Bank loans

If you have set up your business as a registered company, you may prefer to take out a business loan. As mentioned before, this limits your liability if the business fails and cannot repay the debt. Banks offer business loans to companies, partnerships and sole traders. A bank will want to see your business plan, evidence of the funds you are investing in the project, and details of how the business will repay the loan. If your business is already established, include accounts from previous years' trading. Contracts with buyers to purchase your products and services in the future will also strengthen your case for a loan. The bank will probably also want to then hear from you regularly about how the business is performing and whether it is meeting targets.

Dan funded his business a little at a time. He says, "I'd spend a thousand pounds on stock, sell it, then use the proceeds to pay for the next shipment." Dan faced challenges getting more funding for the business. He says, "I was in debt when my wife died. I just didn't have time to think about our finances while I was looking after her and the children. I didn't go bankrupt, but it has still affected my credit record. I feel the banks haven't always wanted to lend me as much as the business needed."

Arabella asked the bank for a loan to help her business get off the ground. She says, "We had a matched amount in our own funds, so the bank was happy to lend us the money." Arabella continues, "My salary varies from month to month. We still reinvest a lot, even after a couple of years in business. I earn enough to pay for holi-days and clothes."

Other investors

You can also look for other sorts of investment. You may have a friend or family member who is willing to make a loan to the business. Make sure you are clear about the terms of repay-ment and what control, if any, the investment gives to the investor. You may be pleased if a relative loans you £5,000 to get started, but less pleased if they then start wanting to know every detail of how you run the business. Clarify things like this in writing before accepting loans.

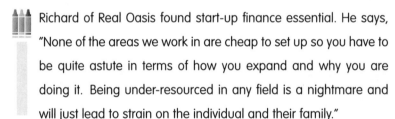

Richard of Real Oasis found start-up finance essential. He says, "None of the areas we work in are cheap to set up so you have to be quite astute in terms of how you expand and why you are doing it. Being under-resourced in any field is a nightmare and will just lead to strain on the individual and their family."

Angel money

You may also get finance from a professional investor, an angel. This sort of investor will be experienced at assessing businesses and business plans. They will be looking for a strong and growing business to give them a return on their money. An angel will probably want part of your company, known as shares or equity, in return for their money, and a say in managing the company.

Venture capital

Finally, if you are looking for large investments to the tune of hundreds of thousands, look into venture capital. City investors will finance a business, in return for a share in the company. This sort of investment will usually depend on your company meeting performance targets and financial goals. The investor may also want a seat on the board of directors.

Profit and pricing

When you are making your business plans, you need to be clear how you will make your company profitable. This applies from the smallest company up. Will you be supplying wholesale? If so, you need to calculate in margins so that your retailers can make a profit. They will want around 50 per cent profit after VAT, and you need to cover your materials, time, marketing and distribution costs too.

 Miranda tries to work smarter rather than harder. She says, "Assess your margins. Don't sell stuff too cheap, make sure that you're covering your costs and making enough to cover overheads. It is pointless running round like a headless chicken if you're not making enough money. It's best to be quieter and sell less at a better margin so that overall you're getting the same money in profit for less work. This will also cut your volume of work so you'll have less stress from the stuff hanging over you.

VAT

Think about VAT registration early on. You need to register

once your turnover exceeds £61,000. This figure increases by a small amount annually, so check current figures. Even if you aren't registered for VAT when you start out, consider allowing for it in your prices. Otherwise, an increase of 17.5 per cent can either be a nasty shock for your customers, or make an unpleasant dent in your profits.

Arabella backdated her business's VAT registration to the website launch. She says, "This meant we had to cover a small period where we weren't charging customers VAT, but as we had lots of investments to get the shop started, registering for VAT still worked out to be beneficial." Some of Arabella's competitors are not registered for VAT. She says, "This makes quite a difference in the pricing. It can be hard to compete with smaller sellers who are not VAT registered. If they are successful they will need to register for and charge VAT too eventually." Arabella has both an online mail order business and a shop. She says, "Occasionally this can cause problems with pricing. Business is competitive on the web and sometimes competitors will offer products with low margins, and we may reduce our web prices so we can compete. This can lead to a difference between the price online and the price in the shop. We try to keep this to a minimum, so customers don't lose out wherever they shop with us."

Payment terms

Plan out your payment terms. Acceptable terms can vary, depending on the sector you work in. A standard invoice may request payment within 30, 60 or even 90 days. Work out your cash flow so your customers pay you in time for you to pay your bills. Will you need an overdraft at some times of the year? If you are dealing with large amounts of money coming in and out, you may need to look at debt factoring. You sell your invoices on to a company which will give you in the region of 85 per cent of their value straight away. They then take on responsibility for chasing up the payment, for a fee. This gives you access to money you are owed more quickly, but obviously at a price. Consult a solicitor before setting up this sort of arrangement.

Your income

If the family will be relying on your business, you need to establish the income you draw from the business. Make this part of your business plan. Some people plan in a regular 'salary' of a fixed amount each month, while others take whatever is left, or what they need.

 Dan of Onya Bags says, "After the first few months of grieving for my wife, I found myself wondering what to do. I did not want to just be at home, but as a single parent needed to be flexible. I also wanted to make a difference to the children and their world." Dan's brother suggested he try selling Onya bags in the UK. Dan's finances were tight. He managed to get the business going with a loan of a few thousand pounds from his other brother. He says, "I got a widower's pension. I was on a 'back to work' scheme so I was allowed to keep my benefits for the first six months while I was setting up. This was vital. I put every penny that the business made back into developing Onya Bags, and only started taking money about a year down the line."

Liz started Power Pramming with the aim of being able to pay half of the family's bills. She says, "It took a while but I have built up classes and personal clients. Good media coverage has helped. My classes take place in a park, and a group of mums with buggies doing exercises is visible, which helps word spread too. It's taken a couple of years but I have met my financial goals, and can see how the business can grow even further." Liz now has a couple of other mums who also run classes for her, and is investigating the possibility of extending this to other areas or developing a franchise scheme.

Where will you work?

If you are taking your business seriously, think carefully about where you will locate it. Will you be able to run the business from home? Do you have a garage that could be converted or is there space for a garden office? If you plan to work from home, review after a few years or months, and see how having a business in your house is affecting family life. It can make it hard to close the door on work at the end of the day, and put a strain on relationships.

 Dan started with a stall at a local market. He would drop the children off, and then rush to set up, incurring jibes from other stall holders who had been there for an hour or more already. Dan visited Greenwich market and decided that a stall there would give him a much bigger market, reaching thousands of Londoners and tourists each week. He says, "I used to drop the kids at my mother-in-law's on a Friday night, and sleep on a friend's floor in London. I'd be up early and work all day Saturday and Sunday at the market, then collect the children around 9pm on Sunday evening."

Sam and Jean still use an office in Jean's home, which has advantages and disadvantages. Jeans says, "Sam has to drive to work, while I don't have a journey, but it's harder for me to switch off at the end of the day. I find I work on days I plan to take off. As the office is in my home, I need to take the kids out if Sam is working."

Getting premises

Running the business from home may not be for you, or you may have started at home and need more space. Research your options carefully. Where do you want your premises to be located? What sort of passing trade do you need? Think about the sort of advertising you will need to do to attract customers to your premises. You may want to pick somewhere that is handy for home, or within easy reach of your children's school. Consider whether it is best to buy or rent. If you want to rent, are you looking for a long or short lease? You can negotiate on rent in the same way as you might negotiate the price on a house purchase. And, just as with a house purchase, make sure you get professional help before signing a lease. When costing your premises, work out how much you will need for a deposit, and factor in business rates and utilities.

Tracey and Nik Hand each have their own businesses. Tracey has been running Budget Bumps for six years. Nik has moved gradually from working full-time, to being employed part-time and spending the rest of his time building up Jesters Trick Bits, selling motorcycle body parts. In the last year, Nik took redundancy to work on his business full-time, and both businesses have moved into premises. Tracey says, "Work needed to move out of the home. I started with a few boxes of maternity wear but the house was overrun, and it affected us all." Tracey started looking for shops, and viewed six different properties without finding the right one. She continues, "Some were in a great location, but expensive, while others were in terrible condition, or didn't have space for stock. Budget Bumps does lots of mail order, so I needed room for packing too." In the meantime, Nik hit it lucky. He explains, "A friend had a garage building with a showroom, which became vacant. I wasn't looking for premises as actively as Tracey, but this opportunity was too good to miss. It gave me the chance to move the business into a great space, without being tied to a long lease." Once Nik was sorted, Tracey found an alternative to viewing further shops. She says, "I found an office at a business and enterprise centre. I weighed up the costs compared to a shop. The rent covers heat, lighting, telephone and even broadband. I signed up for an annual contract, with the option of a month's notice at any time. It was a nice idea to have a shop, but actually my money is better invested promoting the business online. Here I achieve a higher turnover with lower overheads and without increased staffing costs. My office is more flexible while the children are small. If I need to collect one of them from school because of sickness, I can transfer the phone, lock the door and dash off. It is nice being amongst other businesses too. I hadn't realised how isolating it could be working at home." Moving business out of the home has worked well for the Hands. Nik says, "Our house looks like a home again. The kids have the old office to play in." Tracey adds, "It's great being able to go to work and come home at the end of the day. The business centre closes in the evening. I sometimes bring my laptop home, but there's no temptation to spend the evening sorting boxes of stock, and Nik is no longer out in the garage working on bikes."

Arabella Greatorex started Natural Nursery as an online and mail order business, but opened a shop within six months. She says, "A shop wasn't always in the plan, but we took our natural baby products to local fairs and farmers' markets. Again and again people asked if we had a shop. There was only one natural baby shop in Bristol, on the other side of town, so I took the idea seriously. It soon became clear that there was one street in our area that would suit such a shop. I was worried that if we didn't start up, another baby business would. The area had improved enormously over the previous decade and there were lots of young families moving in. So I took a short lease on the first shop that came up in the right location. A few months later we moved to permanent premises just a few doors down, and have committed to a standard 15-year lease." Arabella admits that starting a shop so soon was not perfect timing for her personally, but feels that the business reasons were compelling enough to make her act.

Shop design and fitting

If you are taking on premises, think about the interior. Do you need desks, special equipment, or simply good display areas for customers? Include this in the finances when writing your business plan.

Arabella says, "Our shop is simple. We wanted something friendly and open. There was also a need to fit the shop out ethically to
go with the green ethos of the shop. We have organic paper on
the wall. Our fittings came from Ikea, who have strict ethical
controls."

Stock and storage

One further element to choosing a location for your business
is considering what you will do with stock. How much storage
space will your business need? It can be expensive to find large
premises, so many businesses have separate storage away from
prime retail sites. Equally, if you are basing your business in
the home, storage can be critical. Think about the volume of
stock you will hold, and where it will go.

 Arabella says, "We had a lot of stock when we were an online
business, and now we have the shop too we also have a 2000
square foot storage unit which fortunately is just across the road.
We have a stock control system, but however careful we try to be,
there are still occasional discrepancies."

Stuart and Lynda keep Free Range Kids' stock in a rented storage
area, and Stuart goes down there a couple of times a week. He
says, "I bring back enough for the next couple of days' orders, so
the house isn't too full of boxes. We have stock in the storage facility to meet larger wholesale orders too. I try to minimise the time
and cost of travelling there though."

Miranda says, "Assess your stock. Anything not selling? Drop the
price to clear. It is pointless clogging up the place with stock

that won't sell and just takes up space. I publicise sales well. Customers love a bargain, and usually add in some non-sale items too." Miranda continues, "See if you can find a place to store non-essential boxes. We had a corner of a granary on a farm for a while. Can you buy a shed for the garden? Or does a neighbour have a spare bit of garage for a few pounds a week? Reclaim some home space. It made a great difference to me when we first moved some stock out, and then finally moved the whole business."

Staff

Will you need staff when your business expands? It can seem daunting taking on employees. You may want to start with staff on a casual or freelance basis. Be clear, if you are doing this, what basis you are employing someone under, and who is responsible for their tax and national insurance. HM Revenue and Customs has a guide about working on a freelance basis which will help you establish whether someone is self-employed.

Becoming an employer

At some point, as your business grows, you will need a permanent employee. HM Revenue and Customs has information on taking people on, and you will also need to contact HMRC to register as an employer.

Arabella of Natural Nursery has one full-time member of staff, two part-timers and a woman who does ad hoc cover. She says, "I work three full and three half days. Lisa, our 'cover' lady is essential. She comes in to cover holiday, and we know she can help if anyone is sick." Having staff is not always easy. Arabella continues, "The thing I enjoy least is staff management."

Taking husband Rod on as an employee has made Michaela realise that it wasn't difficult to become an employer. She says, "You can fill in most of the details on a disk now. We have since taken on a machinist who works here four hours a day. This is more efficient than using outworkers: there's no need to deliver cut nappies for sewing. Often we'd find the outworkers ran out of something like labels, which they forgot to collect. We'd then have to spend more time dropping extra items round to them."

Trade and consumer shows

Attending events is a vital part of reaching out to customers. Trade shows can help you reach new contacts for wholesale accounts, and consumer shows can put your business in front of people who you wouldn't reach in other ways. If you are selling from home, a regular programme of shows and exhibitions may be a good option instead of a shop. Weigh up the show fees versus the costs of a permanent shop.

 Laura Park of BrightSpark Slings is a veteran of parenting shows. She shares her tips: "Plan your stand ahead. I tape off a square on my office floor and mock up my stand so I know what I am doing when I reach the venue. I try to have at least two people on the stand. This allows one of you to have a rest or go to the loo. Don't be shy about approaching people: they are there to spend money or gather information and if you get them with your unique selling point they are usually caught for long enough to give them your spiel. I take plenty of flyers. It makes people slow down for a second so you can get your unique selling point in, and gives people a visual reminder of your product. I also take water and snacks. It is thirsty work talking all day, and you may not have time for much of a lunch break." Laura also recommends wearing comfortable clothes and shoes. She says, "We have company T-shirts for staff. We ordered a small run from **www.hesays shesays.co.uk**. On a busy stand they make it obvious who is staff and who is a customer. Take an emergency kit too. Pack sticky tape, sticky pads, sewing kit, scissors, string, paper clips: you never know when you will need them." Laura also takes information for wholesalers, and a sign for the stand inviting trade enquiries. Laura has her prices on display, because, she says, "People may pass by because they don't want to ask how much things are." Demonstrations and trials are a key part of any show that Laura attends. She says, "People are much more likely to buy something if they have tried it for themselves. With baby carriers, people may have fears about safety or comfort. It is important to reassure them, and trying the sling can convince them." Laura tries to have a special offer at each show, offering incentives for people to purchase on the day. She adds, "If possible, round your prices down to the nearest £5. You won't then need a complicated float, but make sure you have plenty of fivers as change."

Michaela says, "We went to a trade show at the NEC. I'm glad I did it because it changed how the business was perceived. It took Nappies by Minki from being a kitchen table business to a brand.

It was hard work though, and difficult to set up as it was such a distance from home on the Hebrides."

Stuart attends trade shows on a regular basis. He says, "I'm going to the two major trade shows this year. It is nice going back annually as you always find someone you've met before to mind your stall or socialise with. And I've got far more experience in making sure I get a good pitch." Although it can seem expensive, Stuart says, "If you can find two or three good wholesale customers you can cover the cost of your stand with their purchases over a year. And the more you visit shows the more use you get out of display equipment and posters, even if they are costly to start." Stuart follows up leads from shows, but without being pushy. He says, "Our aim is to build good relationships with small independent shops. We are aiming for gentle organic growth and a good long-term relationship helps. Store owners may see you at two or three shows before buying. If we can add a couple more retailers each month we will achieve the growth we are after without suddenly having to cope with a massive increase in workload."

This chapter touches on only a few of the issues you might face if you want your business to grow. Visit your local Enterprise Agency or Business Link for further advice.

Chapter 9

How to guide

If you want to follow the examples of some of the busy and successful people you have read about, here are a few steps to get you started on planning for a business of your own.

Check out your market

Develop a few ideas about what you want to offer, and then ask yourself whether there is a market for it. Before you invest time and money in the business check out the competition. For example, if you want to make and sell a craft item, go round the local craft fairs and shops and see what other people are selling. How much are they charging, and how does that compare to the cost of your time and materials if you were to make something similar? Is anyone offering something identical to what you were going to do, and if so, are you able to cover different geographical areas or is there something else that will set you apart? Look on the internet – eBay and other websites can help you see how much similar items are selling for.

Market research

When you are working out your plans for your business, it helps if you have a clear idea about who you are trying to reach and what they want. You can find out a lot by asking people about your products or services. Use interviews or surveys to get feedback on whether they might buy, and if not, why not.

What sort of research?

Start by deciding how best to do your research. You could interview people, one-to-one. This sort of interview is good if you want to discuss sensitive topics such as finances or health. Alternatively, get a group of about eight existing or potential customers together and spend an hour chatting through a prepared list of topics. This is called a focus group. Record interviews and go back to listen to what people say. It will help you draw out in depth thoughts on your business. If you want to get a wider range of views, try a survey. Offer a voucher or discount as an incentive to get people to participate.

Surveys

Whichever method you use, make sure you have a simple form asking people about their age, sex, income, and where they live. This helps you work out which groups of people have different views. Ask about which papers and magazines they read in case you want to advertise or send out press releases later. Then, ask about products, services and pricing. Find out people's opinions on how the business is delivered: do they have a preference for ways to pay, how to buy or order etc. Trial the questions on friends to ensure that everything is clear.

Research now can save you hundreds or thousands of pounds. Test your market before you invest money in your business to save making expensive mistakes.

Planning

Once you have done a little market research, plan what to do next. Why not make or buy in some of the items you want to sell? If you are making something, work out exactly how long it takes and how much it costs you. Then look at different ways to sell it. You could put something on eBay, or ask whether friends would be interested in buying. At this stage you are really just sounding out the market. It is important to see if your item will sell at a reasonable price, which leaves you some profit, before getting into larger scale production or investing heavily in materials.

Test your pricing

Similarly, if you are going to offer a service, have a few trial runs with friends and relatives. Try out your pricing, and remember to factor in the materials you use or costs like travel.

How much time do you have?

If you think your idea will sell, now work out how busy you

want to be. Do you want to have enough work to be busy during school hours, or build up stock to sell at a craft fair every few months? Are there key times of year when people will buy your products – Christmas, Valentine's day, or year round for birthdays. You should also have a good idea of how long it takes you to create your items or provide your service, and how much time you can commit to the business.

What are your business aims?

Work out your aims for the business, and this will help you make sure you stay in control and enjoy what you are doing. Now is a good time to start making a simple business plan. This does not have to be complex if you are using it for your own purposes. Business plans usually include the following sections:

- A description of your enterprise and what you want to do

- What you are offering and how it will appeal to customers

- Your market – who you will be selling to, how you will reach them

- What you will do and when – a more detailed breakdown of activities and dates

Finance

You should also make a simple financial plan. This could just start with the costs of your materials and expenses. As the business grows you might also want to look at profit and loss, cash flow, balance sheet, break-even analysis. Talk to a business adviser at your local Enterprise Agency for more help with finances.

You may feel that this is lots of detail if you are just selling a few items, but proper planning can save you from making a loss, and help you improve what you do in the future. It is also easier to start noting down expenses and building a list of customer names now. It can take a lot of valuable time to catch up if you wait until business is booming.

Business banking

Think about setting up a business banking account. Many banks now offer free start-up business banking. It enables you to separate business expenses from personal ones easily. If you need some start-up capital, you may want to make a loan to the business from your personal funds. Note this down, and the business can repay your investment, however small, as you make profits.

Insurance

Make sure you think about insurance. Firstly, check that your household buildings and contents insurance still covers you once you are running a business from home. This should not be a problem if you are using a limited part of the house, and do not have business visitors. If you have clients coming to your house you will need public liability insurance, to protect you if, for example, someone fell while in your house. The insurance company may also be able to provide you with cover if someone was injured while using one of your products.

Equipment insurance

You may need to get extra insurance for equipment. If you have a computer that is largely for home use, it will probably still be covered by your home contents insurance, but if you buy an industrial sewing machine, say, specifically for business it is unlikely that this will be covered. Some insurance companies provide specific 'working from home' policies which cover your need for domestic buildings and contents insurance, as well as business contents, employer's liability, public liability, products liability and legal expenses.

Finally, if you use your car to transport business items, to a craft fair, for example, check whether this is covered by your motor insurance. You may simply need to let them know that you are doing this.

More insurance

People providing services may need professional indemnity (PI) insurance. This covers your business if you act in a professional capacity. In some professions, such as accountancy, taking out PI cover is a legal requirement. If you have people working for you, you will need employer's insurance. This protects your business against claims from employees for accidents and sickness, for example. Limited company directors may want director's insurance, which protects against being sued for negligence, for example. Legal expenses insurance covers court costs and legal fees. Always check with your own insurance company about your circumstances. Information given in this book is to illustrate the issues only.

Promotion

Your business promotion can make or break your enterprise. There are many people with fabulous products or services who struggle to make their business pay due to lack of customers. Write down a list of all the different ways you can promote your business, and try to do at least one thing each day.

 Richard Boyd says, "Understand how to market your business – you can be brilliant at what you do but if no one knows about you, you might as well not bother."

Liz promotes her classes by mentioning them to anyone pushing a pram, and talking to mother and baby groups. She says, "Pregnancy and baby magazines have contacted me for advice on exercise routines for new mums. I always provide something even though there is no payment, as it really gets your brand known."

Organise to grow

These are some of the main issues you will need to address when planning a business. Whether you are thinking about finances, staff, promotion or other admin, keep good records from day one. Record all your transactions, start a day book for notes, a file for receipts, and it will help you stay in control of your new business as it grows.

Chapter 10

When you're struggling

It is not always easy to work and look after the family. This chapter looks at some of the issues you might face. Juggling kids, your business and having a life can be much harder than you realise. When things go well it's all down to you and that's a fantastic feeling. Read on to find how other parents have coped with challenges in home and business life, and get advice on how to deal with childcare crises, lack of sleep, and lack of hours in the day.

Housework

Many of the things that may get you down will be boring and domestic. Many working parents find that they are so busy there is no time to do housework. It can be difficult to work from home when home is a mess, and children have little thought of picking up after themselves. Try to work out a routine for cleaning that doesn't leave everything to you. Some people spend a few minutes on one room each day. Cleaning the bathroom on Monday, the lounge on Tuesday and so on means that you don't have to do the whole house, and ensures that each room gets a turn.

Chuck your clutter

It is easier to clean if you have less stuff. Throw out broken toys, be ruthless about recycling, and have a box for the charity shop which you put unwanted items into. Visit US site **www.flylady.net** for more cleaning routines and decluttering tips.

 Miranda has run her own business for eight years, since the birth of her daughter. She has lots of tips and experiences to share. She says, "I try to do one tidying house task on the way to doing something else. If the post has arrived I open it all and put as much as I can in the right place, recycle envelopes and junk mail so that all that is in 'pending' is the bills. If I notice the loo roll needs changing I do it while I'm in the bathroom and stuff the empty loo roll in the bin. If the bin is full I do a slight detour to empty it into the main bin. Involve the kids in cleaning and tidying too. Turn it into a game like 'Let's see how many blue bits of Lego we can count into the bucket, now how many red,' or arm them with a small duster and give them tasks."

Time saving tips

If you're working more, you will need more help with all the other jobs round the house. Work out ways to make it easier at critical times of the day, and make other members of the family pull their weight.

Have a second set of toothbrushes and paste downstairs to save crucial moments in the morning. If the children brush their teeth in the cloakroom or kitchen you can keep an eye on them, whereas if they wander off upstairs it can take precious minutes to get them back on track for school.

Take turns cooking the evening meal. Get the kids involved. Ask them each to be responsible for one night of the week. Even if the six year old can only make sandwiches, it won't hurt anyone to eat them for one night, and they can soon progress to beans on toast. Older kids will enjoy being responsible for one meal, as long as they get lots of praise whatever the results. Give everyone responsibilities for clearing up afterwards too.

When you cook, double your quantities if it is a meal that will freeze. You'll then save time on cooking another night of the week.

 Sharon of HeSaysSheSays says, "I find getting up an hour earlier to deal with emails, check Statcounter, and do any small jobs helps enormously. Then I get ready for the day before the kids are up."

Richard Boyd says, "Everyone in business today is time poor, so good time management is paramount to becoming successful."

Money

Whatever work you do, it is likely that there will be times when money is stretched, whether it is because you are only able to fit in a few hours of work round the children, or because you are investing everything you can in expanding your business. There is no easy solution to this. Prepare as much as you can by putting a few pounds aside each week against tax if you are self-employed. You should also check that you are paying the correct National Insurance contributions. Paying in, even if your income is below the threshold, will give you access to benefits like Maternity Allowance.

Budget beaters

There are plenty of websites that will help with budgeting – Money Saving Expert is probably the best known. Watch out for tips to help you plan economical meals, and use a shopping list so you don't spend on unnecessary items. Sign up to your local Freecycle too. It is a great way to recycle your unwanted items, and will help you find items you need at no cost.

 Liz says, "Of course, not everything is great financially when you are setting up a business. My pension has been put on hold. I worry slightly every time my former pension company get in touch that I need to start paying in again."

Time for the kids

You may feel that although you want to be there for the kids, often business takes over. And if it's your own business there may be no one else to cover. Cut yourself a bit of slack. There will be days when you need to put on a DVD and set the kids up with a pile of snacks to watch something quietly so you can work. Deal with the guilt by reminding yourself of all the times you are there at school or nursery events, and the times you can be at home when they are sick. Read on for more ideas about how other working parents find time for the family.

 Miranda aims to play with her daughter first. She says, "Spend the morning doing something energetic and fun. Go for a walk, to the park, swimming. This is fun for them and, importantly, tiring. When you stuff them with food at lunch if they're young they'll nap, if not they're happy to chill with a DVD and interrupt you less. A bit of fresh air and exercise will motivate you, and make you feel better, meaning when you do work you'll be 200% more efficient so it won't matter you took two hours out earlier." Miranda also recommends having kids over in the school holidays. "My staff have school-age children too. Some days it can seem like a holiday camp here, but they get on with playing together and one of us can supervise while the others work."

Karen says, "Set time aside to be a mum. After school play with your child or help with homework. Whenever possible I take and collect my children from school. On the 25-minute journey, I have time to hear about their day and my time is just focused on the children – no phone calls, email or supper to deal with."

Liz's success has been achieved by fitting work into nap times, evenings and weekends. She says, "It gets easier when your child starts nursery – I had a couple of hours each morning free to work." Liz's plans for expansion had to be put on hold temporarily while she took a brief maternity break after the birth of her second child. She says, "I hadn't realised how much I got done while my son was at nursery. Now I'm back to a day where the baby can make demands at any time, and I have to look after a toddler too."

Bex says, "For me I tend to do children things during the day, then work at night – this doesn't work for everyone, but it does mostly for me."

Cathie's tip is, "Never be too busy for a book, a game, a hug."

Childcare

However you work, good childcare really helps. If your children are at school, plan what you will do during the school holidays. Most parents will welcome the chance to spend time with the children, but planning to swap play dates one or more days a week can help you stay on top of business too. Look at local play schemes, twist the arms of relatives, and arrange work so you can take some time off too.

Early years

If you have pre-schoolers things can be a bit more complicated. If you are really lucky you will have relatives who can help with regular or back-up childcare. Otherwise, your local authority will be able to fill you in on childminders and nurseries in your area. You will need to think through how you will manage work if your child is sick and cannot attend their regular childcare.

 Karen says, "It was personally right for me to fit Musical Minis around my children and not the children around Musical Minis.

This meant I would finish classes a week before the end of my children's nursery term at Christmas, so I would be able to go to their Christmas shows." With regard to childcare, Karen continues, "Have back-up. If your child is ill what will happen to your business? I would have to phone someone to run the class on my behalf."

Vanessa says, "Childcare is an enormous cost: half my earnings after tax. We have 'solved' our childcare issue by getting our priorities straight. Our daughter comes first, so we forgo the guilt and know that nothing is important enough in our jobs to not stay home and care for her." Vanessa has worked out a back-up plan, with a friend who will look after her daughter if it is absolutely essential. She says, "Developing a back-up network of care should be a top priority for new parents. Without relatives it is a matter of befriending neighbours, getting involved with your local NCT, making friends in antenatal groups, being a part of Netmums, and prioritising friendships so you have a support community when you need."

Work and home crises

However carefully you plan, there will be times when you have to put work to one side and deal with a family crisis. Be realistic about this from the start. If you are working for yourself, this is one of the times that you need to make the most of the flexibility you have. If you have staff, make sure that they are able to cope with day-to-day tasks to keep the business running. If everything is done by you, just make sure someone communicates with your customers that there may be a delay. Most people will understand that they are dealing with a small business, especially if you explain that there are delays due to sickness or bereavement, for example.

 Cathie says, "Be honest and up front with people. If you are struggling or your children are ill, explain. Many customers will value your honesty."

Bex says, "When I get big orders or have short deadlines I have a number of people I can call on for childcare, and also a core of sewing people that I can call on at short notice to help with stitching."

Work-life balance

It is easy to let running your own business take over your life, especially if you work evenings and weekends. Suddenly you can find that you have no hobbies or social life, and rarely relax with your partner as you are too busy working. Try to have regular time when you don't work. Make Friday night a night off with a DVD or bottle of wine.

 Emily says, "Look at your work-life balance. It is easy to spend too much time on one or the other."

Karen aims to separate work from home, "If your business is based at home have a second phone line fitted. If you're bathing the children, for example, the answer machine will pick up the call. If a child is having a tantrum you don't have to speak about business and get more stressed. Phone back once the children are settled."

Miranda tries to finish working 15 minutes before school-run time, saying, "I find this hard to do, but it does make me more productive. I force myself not to answer the phone, but instead to tidy the desk area and sort the chaos that has accumulated while I'm working. Then I decide what I have to do tomorrow, write a list and prioritise it. I like to make sure there are lots of short easy ones on there. Then the next day I can zip through the list and get on with it quickly. Being able to cross off lots of small points will make you feel good."

Cathie says, "Have a separate area for your work so you can put it away or close the door on it until the next day."

Nadine says, "If I'm feeling low it is a great time to count my blessings and write down the positives of working for yourself – how nice it is to have a satisfied customer, buying new stock, sourcing new lines, no office politics, being able to eat what you want when you want and take as many loo trips as you need. Then the flip side of this is that this way of life is not for everyone. Working out what you would do instead may be a great motivation to continue."

Me time

Even if you are working for yourself, there will be times when you get sick of work. If you can, take a break. Have a few hours off or a day out, even if it is one of the days you normally work. Alternatively, spend some time tidying the house or playing with the kids. To keep yourself motivated, make sure you plan in some regular time for yourself. If there is a hobby you love, plan to spend some time on it each week.

 Karen says, "Set time aside for you. Running a business and having a family gives you no free time – there is always something you should be doing. It is important, whenever possible, to give you time to relax – maybe meet a friend for lunch, go shopping for yourself."

When to quit

Although most problems can be overcome not every parent working for themselves will go on doing so indefinitely. Some people are happy to go back to paid work once their children are in full-time school, while others close their business for personal reasons.

 Emma has run a busy franchise for a number of years. The birth of her son has made her rethink. She says, "I went along to classes with my daughter, now six, and ended up buying the franchise. During the last three years I have enjoyed being my own boss and arranging classes to suit the needs of my family. I am now selling, as I can't give enough time to the business without missing my new baby growing up. I would definitely consider going back to a business like this when he starts school."

Lynne Laverty ran a successful children's clothing company. She found it increasingly hard to put time into the business after it became evident her son had special needs. She says, "The business took off quicker that I expected. It got to the point that I had to squeeze everything in at the last moment. Things got more difficult with Logan. He wasn't sleeping. I'd get him settled and sit down to sew at 11.30pm. Something had to give, Logan needed my attention. I started the business as something for me but it got to the point where I wasn't enjoying it. Five months after his diagnosis with autism, I knew I couldn't physically do it, and I wanted to give the kids priority. It was the right thing to do. Part of me wishes I could have kept it going, but it was just the wrong time. A friend took the business over. I'm glad that someone is running it, as it is a successful business. I might start my own business again, and will have more time to give to something when the kids are settled at school."

Bex says, "I have had lows where all I want to do is throw in the towel but have come out the other side glad that I am still working on something that keeps me sane. If I feel like that I get out for a few hours with the kids – they love it, and I do too."

One-man band?

One of the biggest challenges of starting a business is having to do everything yourself. While a few start-ups budget for big premises and employed staff right from the beginning, many more grow organically. Read the experiences of the parents below, which are packed with tips for coping with the multi-tasking required when you run your own business.

 Chris says, "If you set up in business, you are the only person to do all of the roles from marketing to filing to accounts to being the telephonist. It's a real work in progress. Working for someone else on a salary is much easier."

Karen advises, "Know your limitations. For example if you have problems with accounts get someone to help you. If there are not enough hours in the day to do everything, do the bits you like and get help with the bits you don't. Get a cleaner or shop online. Set time aside to deal with admin, household tasks etc. If you keep putting it off the task will become huge. It will be daunting to be faced by hours of paperwork or loads of ironing. Regular manageable chunks of mundane but important tasks will help things flow smoothly."

Miranda says, "Contemplate taking on a packer/bookkeeper/cleaner/washer-up/Girl Friday for five to six hours a week initially to do mundane but time-consuming jobs. There are hordes of people who want a local child-friendly job that fits in with a school run. As long as you pay the same as Tesco or Asda in most areas they'll be far happier as you will be offering school-friendly hours. Then when they are 'doing' you can also 'do', which doubles the amount of stuff done. Overall the cost is minimal and really won't break the bank unless you've not marked up your product lines sufficiently. Think you can't afford it? How much business are you losing out on if you are not sending goods out quickly enough? We notice an upsurge in repeat orders if we get the stock out quickly."

Succeeding in business

There are many challenges that you will face while running your own business. This book can cover only a few examples, but every business will have its own unique issues. The best advice is to get some support. Make an appointment with Business Link or a similar enterprise agency, join a networking group, or log on to one of the many business forums online.

 Lucy McGowan of Chutney Beads says, "Be patient. Success does not come overnight and you need to work, work, work!"

Conclusion

If you have read right through this book, I hope you are full of ideas about how to change your working life so you have a better balance and can spend the time you want with the family.

If you have a job, but want to change your hours, approach your employer. If they aren't keen to change, tell them about the great things you do for the business, and explain how you can see your contribution continuing, or even improving, with a new working pattern. If you still have no luck, start looking around. There are jobs out there with flexible hours. Visit websites like **www.workingmums.co.uk** and **www.mumand working.co.uk** to find more opportunities – despite the names, most opportunities also are available to dads who want flexible or part-time jobs too.

If you are now full of entrepreneurial spirit and want to start your own business, get planning. It is far easier to set a business up properly in the beginning. Look for business plan templates online and work through each section. You may not need a full plan to start off with, but it will help you to take a systematic look at issues such as the market and marketing, premises, finance, staff and legal requirements. Make the most of support from business development staff at local Enterprise Agencies too.

Whatever you are doing, find some support, either locally or online. Networking and building friendships with other business owners can be a lifesaver. There is probably a networking group in your area meeting for breakfast, lunch or an evening drink, so you'll be able to find a time to network that fits with the family. Finding other people doing the same as you online means you can get support even when you're tied up at home with the children.

Seize the moment to change your life for the better, and make the most of your time while your family is growing up. Your kids will value the extra time you have to spend with them enormously. You will be able to look at your working life and family and be proud of what you are achieving.

Useful Contacts

You'll find plenty of useful addresses, website links and contact numbers on our website at **www.whiteladderpress.com** to make it easier for you to access them, and for us to keep them updated. Just click on 'Useful contacts' next to the information about this book. If you don't have internet access, contact us via any of the methods listed on this page and we'll print off a copy and post it to you free of charge.

Contact us

You're welcome to contact White Ladder Press if you have any questions or comments for either us or the author. Please use whichever of the following routes suits you.

Phone 01803 813343 between 9am and 5.30pm

Email enquiries@whiteladderpress.com

Fax 01803 813928

Address White Ladder Press, Great Ambrook, Near Ipplepen, Devon TQ12 5UL

Website www.whiteladderpress.com

What can our website do for you?

If you want more information about any of our books, you'll find it at **www.whiteladderpress.com**. In particular you'll find extracts from each of our books, and reviews of those that are already published. We also run special offers on future titles if you order online before publication. And you can request a copy of our free catalogue.

Many of our books also have links pages, useful addresses and so on relevant to the subject of the book. You'll also find out a bit more about us and, if you're a writer yourself, you'll find our submission guidelines for authors. So please check us out and let us know if you have any comments, questions or suggestions.

Sneaky Parenting

Smart shortcuts to  happy families

Jo Wiltshire

Are you a perfect parent? A yummy mummy or a delicious dad? Or are there days when you feel more like a stale, worn out shell, struggling to do the best for your child? Feed them 5-a-day, play games with them, keep their minds stimulated, bath them, read to them, wash their clothes, and still have a life of your own...

Luckily, it's perfectly possible to be a brilliant parent without being a perfect one. You just need to know all the sneaky tips, tricks and strategies that Jo Wiltshire has collected from loads of real parents. Parents who care more whether the kids are happy than whether their clothes are clean. That way you'll be able to give your child everything they need without draining yourself dry in the process.

You'll find countless clever shortcuts and real life tricks in here to help look after your baby, toddler or pre-schooler:

- mealtimes
- holidays
- minor illnesses
- messiness
- potty training
- getting dressed
- cleanliness
- grandparents
- sibling rivalry
- socialising
- manners
- baby equipment

If you want a fast track to a happy family, this is it. The book that tells you how to deal with the real stuff – quickly, with humour, and in time for a cup of tea with EastEnders.

£7.99

HOW TO SURVIVE THE TERRIBLE TWOS

Diary of a mother under siege

CAROLINE DUNFORD

Living with a two-year-old isn't necessarily easy. In fact, your child's second year is as steep a learning curve for you as it is for them. While they're finding out about the world, you're struggling to get to grips with everything from food fads to potty training, sleepless nights to choosing a playgroup.

Caroline Dunford has charted a year in the life of her two-year-old son, aptly known as the Emperor on account of his transparent master plan to bend the known universe to his will. She recounts her failures as honestly as her successes, and passes on what she's learnt about:

- how to get a decent night's sleep
- coaxing a half decent diet down your toddler
- keeping your child safe, at home and beyond
- getting your child out of nappies
- curing bad habits, from spitting and hitting to hair pulling and head-banging

...and plenty more of the everyday sagas and traumas that beset any parent of a two-year-old. This real life account reassures you that you're not alone, and gives you plenty of suggestions and guidance to make this year feel more like peaceful negotiation than a siege.

Caroline Dunford has previously worked as a psychotherapist, a counsellor, a supervisor, a writer and a tutor – sometimes concurrently. Even working three jobs at once did not, in any way, prepare her for the onset of motherhood. Today she is a mother and, when her son allows, a freelance writer.

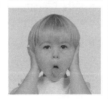

£7.99

Order form

You can order any of our books via any of the contact routes on page 180, including on our website. Or fill out the order form below and fax it or post it to us.

We'll normally send your copy out by first class post within 24 hours (but please allow five days for delivery). We don't charge postage and packing within the UK. Please add £1 per book for postage outside the UK.

Title (Mr/Mrs/Miss/Ms/Dr/Lord etc)

Name

Address

Postcode

Daytime phone number

Email

No. of copies	Title	Price	Total £
Postage and packing £1 per book (outside the UK only):			
TOTAL:			

Please either send us a cheque made out to White Ladder Press Ltd or fill in the credit card details below.

Type of card   ☐ Visa   ☐ Mastercard   ☐ Switch

Card number

Start date (if on card) _____ Expiry date _____ Issue no (Switch) _____

Security code (last 3 digits on reverse of card) _____

Name as shown on card

Signature